# The Bible On
# The Covenant

# The Bible

## on the

## Covenant

by W. BOUWMEESTER

Translated by INGRID VAN LADESTEYN

ST. NORBERT ABBEY PRESS
De Pere, Wisconsin
U. S. A.
1966

Biblical quotations are from the Revised Standard Version of the Bible, copyrighted 1946 and 1952 by the Division of Christian Education, National Council of Churches, and used by permission.

*Nihil obstat:*

    Samuel D. Jadin, O. Praem.
    Censor deputatus

*Imprimatur:*

    †Stanislaus V. Bona, D.D.
    Bishop of Green Bay
    May 22, 1966

    The *Nihil obstat* and *Imprimatur* are a declaration that a book or pamphlet is considered free from doctrinal or moral error. It is not implied that those who have granted the *Nihil obstat* and *Imprimatur* agree with the contents, opinions or statements expressed.

Originally published as
*De Bijbel over het verbond*
Roermond and Maaseik, J. J. Romen & Zonen, 1962

Library of Congress catalogue card number: 66 - 22814

Printed in the United States of America
ST. NORBERT ABBEY PRESS
De Pere, Wisconsin

# CONTENTS

# FOREWORD

"What meaning would you give to the statement that God made a covenant with you?" I once asked a group of young people who had considerable education. The answer was a unanimous disappointing "Nothing!" I had expected something more definite. What, I really could not say. But it should have been more than this apathetic "Nothing."

One might expect that this expression should have some meaning for religiously orientated people, especially in view of the fact that each time the Church celebrates the remembrance of the Passion of Christ, we hear the words of the Lord: Let everybody drink from this cup, for this is my blood, the New and Eternal Covenant, that is shed for you and for many to forgive your sins. We daily commemorate the blood through which Christ established the New Covenant. Each day there is confrontation with it. It would seem natural that at least this would generate an awareness that it is not just another historical fact — like the healing of the blind man of Jericho — but an event with which we all are personally concerned.

Obviously this is not the case, at least not with the great mass of the people and not even with interested religious students. Could the reason be that the concept of covenant has been hidden under a veneer? Or has a feeling of boredom come over us, because in our religion classes we hear over and over again: "In the Old Covenant we had this, in the New Covenant that?"

This book will briefly reflect on what the Bible says about the covenant which God in his mercy made with his people.

# THE COVENANT IN
# EASTERN PERSPECTIVE

The people of Israel possessed traditions in which faith speaks of an almighty and holy God, who breaks through the eternal vaults of heaven to come close to his people. Among these, covenant traditions occupy a prominent place. They tell about God, in his condescending goodness, making alliance with Abraham and his descendants.

We read in Gen. 15:7-18 that Yahweh reveals himself to Abraham: "I am the Lord who brought you from Ur of the Chaldeans to give you this land to possess." He says this to a man who did not own a square inch of the country in which he had just set up his tent. It amazes us that Abraham, although he had great faith, raises a question: "O Lord God, how am I to know that I shall possess it?" The Lord commands him: "Bring me a heifer three years old, a ram three years old, a she-goat three years old, a turtle dove, and a young pigeon. And he brought him all these things, cut them in two, and laid each half over against the other, but he did not cut the birds in two." Yahweh here asks Abraham for an offering. When the sun sets, Abraham sees a flame from the fire-pot passing between these pieces.

It is the Lord; Yahweh is a consuming fire. But when he shows himself to the people, he does so in such a way that the fire is screened by a sort of cloud. The inaccessible God thus makes himself accessible to the people. Genesis tells us that on that day the Lord made a covenant with Abraham saying: "To your descendants I give this land from the river of Egypt to the great river, the river Euphrates."

But this is first realized centuries later! Has Yahweh deluded Abraham? Yahweh anticipates the question and gives the answer in a dream: "Know of a surety that your descendants will be sojourners in a land that is not theirs, and will be slaves there, and they will be oppressed for four hundred years; but I will bring judgment on the nation which they serve, and afterward they shall come out with great possessions. As for yourself, you shall go to your fathers in peace; you shall be buried in a good old age. And they shall come back here in the fourth generations; for the iniquity of the Amorites is not yet complete." Only after centuries will salvation begin to dawn. When iniquity is complete, and Abraham's children cry for help in Egypt, the Lord tells Moses from the midst of a burning bush that he has heard their cries of distress and will bring them to a good and broad land, flowing with milk and honey (Ex. 3:7-8). The Lord summons them to Sinai where he appears again. The description in the Mosaic writings of the events which took place is complicated — the different traditions are so intermingled that it is difficult to distinguish what belongs to the original Yahwist tradition. Yet certain indications can be discerned. We read: "And Mount Sinai was wrapped in smoke, because the Lord descended upon it in fire. Its smoke went up like the smoke of a kiln . . ." This is Yahwist terminology. We have similar expressions in Gen. 15. There the Lord gives the people a sign that he is with them, that he will plead for them as for his brothers. We also note a vestige of the Yahwist tradition in Ex. 24:1-3 and 9-11. The Lord says to Moses: "Come up to the Lord, you and Aaron, Nadab, and Abihu, and seventy of the elders of Israel!" (Ex. 24:1-3). After an interruption the ones called went up and ate and drank in the sight of the Lord (Ex. 24:9-11).

Ex. 34:10-26 is a continuation of the Yahwist tradition. The Lord gives his covenant promise and makes demands of the people: "Behold, I make a covenant with you," he says to Moses. "Before all your people I will do marvels, such as have not been wrought in all the earth or in any nation; and all the people among whom you are shall see the work of the Lord; for it is a terrible thing that I will do with you." He asks faith, to be expressed in worship of the Lord. The ten commandments recorded in Ex. 34:14-26 differ from those we know. They relate only to the worship of Yahweh. The people shall worship no alien god, they shall make no molten gods. They shall keep the feast of unleavened bread. At the time appointed in the month of Abib, the month they came from Egypt, they shall eat unleavened bread for seven days. Every first-born must be brought to Yahweh. But the firstling of an ass can be redeemed, for the Lord knows that they cannot be deprived of this necessary beast of burden. The first-born of the family shall also be redeemed, for Yahweh does not tolerate human sacrifice. The sabbath rest is established. It is worthy to note that the frequently-used explanation of the motivation for this — that God himself also rested on the seventh day — is absent here; this shows that we are within the ancient Yahwist tradition. Then follows the commandment that all males must appear before the Lord three times a year. Finally, rules are made regarding ritual matters. If the people will keep these precepts, the Lord will implement his former promise to Abraham: He will drive out the Amorites, the Canaanites, the Hittites and all other nations before them.

Another ancient tradition tells that Elohim (God) manifested himself on Horeb (Sinai) as He-who-is, and that he again promised to enter into a covenant with the people he led out of Egypt.

The Yahwist tradition holds that God comes with impressive signs: thunder and lightning, a dark cloud over the mountain, trumpet blasts. The people are struck with fear, and stand at a distance, trembling. They say to Moses: "You speak to us, and we will listen; but let not God speak to us, or we will die" (Ex. 20:19). Moses tells them why God has chosen to appear in this manner: ". . . God has come to you only to test you, and put his fear upon you, lest you should sin" (v. 20).

This tradition teaches that God gave the ten commandments on Horeb. These are presented against a background of his revealed majesty. The sacred writings here express an absolute conviction that the ten commandments, the codified natural law, are true laws backed by the full weight of God's omnipotence. The decalog and the covenant book, guidelines for civic, moral and religious life, are the divine basis on which God establishes his covenant with the people. Ex. 24:4-8 describes the solemn covenant ceremony. It tells that Moses sets up memorial pillars with the sacrifices laid on them — burnt offerings to acknowledge God as Lord of everything, peace offerings to celebrate communion with God. It shows how he finally solemnizes the covenant ceremony by sprinkling the sacrificial blood first on the altar and then on the people, who have accepted God's decrees with enthusiasm. "Behold the blood of the covenant which the Lord had made with you in accordance with all these words."

Although the covenant between God and the people had a character all its own — the partners are totally unequal — it would be wrong to consider it as completely different from other pacts made between Eastern peoples. We must see these Old Covenant stories in the general light of the semitic covenant concept.

## 1. In an atmosphere of uncertainty

"O Lord, God, how am I to know that I shall possess it?" asked Abraham in doubt and uncertainty. God's answer was a covenant (Gen. 15:18) which

gives certainty. It is a matter of record, occurring
many times, that a pact is usually born in an atmosphere of mistrust, fear, doubt. Abimelech visits
Abraham to make a covenant because he is afraid
of this stranger who set up his tent near his town,
one with whom he previously had difficulties (Gen.
20); he is afraid because this man has become powerful (Gen. 21:22-33).

Relations were severely strained between Jacob
and Laban. This is clearly shown in the words Jacob
speaks when Laban, his pursuer, overtakes him in
Gilead: "What is my offense? What is my sin, that
you have hotly pursued me? . . . These twenty years
I've been with you, your ewes and your she-goats
have not miscarried, and I have not eaten the rams
of your flocks. That which was torn by wild beasts
I did not bring to you; I bore the loss of it myself;
of my hand you required it, whether stolen by day
or stolen by night. Thus I was; by day the heat
consumed me, and the cold by night; and my sheep
fled from my eyes. These twenty years I have been
in your house; I served you fourteen years for your
two daughters, and six years for your flock, and you
have changed my wages ten times. If the God of
my father, the God of Abraham and the Fear of
Isaac, had not been on my side, surely now you
would have sent me away empty-handed. God saw
my affliction and the labor of my hands, and rebuked
you last night" (Gen. 31:36-42). Under such circumstances Laban thinks it advisable to create a new
atmosphere. "Come now," he says, "let us rather

make a covenant, you and I; and let it be a witness between you and me today" (Gen. 31:44).

It is the same with the Gibeonites who know that they are in desperate straits because not one single fortified town was able to resist Joshua. They too resort to a compact (Jos. 9:1-15; 1 Sam. 11:1-3; 2 Sam. 3:12-13; Hos. 12:2, etc.).

In these cases the initiative came from distressed people. But even when conquerors impose covenants on subjected sovereigns, they expel doubt from their world (1 Kings 20:31-33; Ezek. 17:13-14, etc.). They bind others to themselves to ensure their own position.

An agreement entered into from pure kindness of heart is rare; but here also the result is establishment of a basis for security. This was the case when Jonathan, Saul's son, who loved David "as his own soul" made a covenant with him (1 Sam. 18:1-4).

People like assurance and a covenant gives it. This is especially true when it is made under oath with a heavenly sanction.

## 2. The covenant oath

"Swear to me" Abimelech commands "here by God that you will not deal falsely with me or with my offspring or with my posterity, but as I have dealt loyally with you, you will deal with me and with the land where you have sojourned" (Gen. 21:23). Abraham says: "I will swear" and calls his God to be the witness. A frequently used formula is "God be witness between you and me." In the covenant tradition, with reference to Jacob and Laban, we are told that Jacob sets up a pile of stones. Laban calls it **Mizpah,** which means "watchpost" and says, "The Lord watch between you and me, when we are absent one from the other. If you ill-treat my daughters, or if you take wives besides my daughters, although no man is with us, remember, God is witness between you and me" (Gen. 31:49-50). Because this particular agreement was made in the sight of Yahweh, we read in the later literature of Israel (Samuel and Kings) about covenants made before the face of the Lord (1 Sam. 23:18; 2 Sam. 5:3; 2 Kings 23:3).

A deeply religious people feels certain that Yahweh will take revenge if one of the covenant partners does not keep his word. God is the avenger of a broken pact. Therefore, in the East, it was rather common to express the oath in the form of a curse: "May God do so and so to you and more..." Examples of this are 1 Sam. 3:16-19; 14:43, 44; 25:21, 22, 2 Sam. 3:6-12; 3:35 ff.; 1 Kings 2:21-23; 19:1-4; 20:10; 2 Kings 6:31; Ruth 1:15-17. In Hebrew this is called the **Alah.** The East, with its great love for symbolic language and action, personified this in a tangible way. Here we recall the covenant traditions mentioned in Gen. 15:7-18, as seen above; we are told that the Lord blazed through the animals cut into pieces (cf. Jer. 34:17-18). The explanation is this: "When the inhabitants of Jerusalem had broken their promise, to send away the Hebrew slaves, the oracle of the Lord came over them: You have not obeyed me by proclaiming liberty, every one to his brother and to his neighbor; behold, I proclaim to you liberty to the sword, to pestilence and to famine . . . And the men who transgressed my covenant and did not keep the terms of the covenant which they made before me I will make like the calf which they cut in two and passed between its parts." This explains, in symbolic language, what will happen when one is unfaithful to the covenant. A similar rite was also known to the Assyrians. We are told that the grand-duke Assurnirari, who occupied the throne in Assyria about 750, made a pact with Mati-ilu of Bit-Agusi, who founded an empire in Arpad. The latter was to send him auxiliaries for battle and dedicate offerings to him. Should he not meet his obligations, a curse will strike him, his family, the great men of his people, the army and his country. A ceremony is performed on the occasion of taking this oath: a he-goat is brought and killed. Portentous words are spoken: "This he-goat is not brought here to be offered, but in order to show that Mati-ilu will accept the obligations imposed by Assurnirari, king of Assyria. If Mati-ilu violates these obligations, he, with his sons, daughters, and the people of his country will be carried away, never to return to stand at the head of his country, just as this he-goat, which has been taken out of the flock, never will return to the flock again to hold place of pride. This head is not the head of the he-goat, but Mati-ilu's head, the head of his sons, of the people of the country. If Mati-ilu does not meet the obligations his head will be cut off, like the head of this he-goat has been cut off . . ." Next a series of maledictions follows: "sin and Adad (gods) are allowed to strike Mati-ilu and his subjects with leprosy and famine, their field and cattle are allowed to be infertile, so that they are eating their own sons and daughters; they are to eat dust, and to drink urine."[1]

Similar ceremonies are a probable source of the Hebrew expression **Karat berit,** always translated "making a covenant." The literal meaning is "cutting a covenant." This is a reduction of "to cut an animal into pieces, in order to make a covenant."

The covenant oath distinguishes itself from the witness oath in that it binds the partners together. Here we have the essence of the compact: a relationship is established between the participants which makes mutual trust possible. This would seem to prove the claim of well-known linguists (W. F. Albright, Th. Vriezen, E. Vogt)[2] that the Hebrew **berit** is derived from the Akkadic **biritu** (bond, chain, fetters).

The partners inform each other that they wish to mutually agree in the future and that they endorse the promise they have made with their whole being. The essence of the agreement is therefore friendship, fraternity and fidelity.

### 3.  The essence of the covenant

The Scandinavian scientist J. Pedersen, who made a study[3] of the covenant concept among Bedouin tribes of the Arabian peninsula — tribes of semitic origin — noticed that these people base all protection, all rights and duties on relationship. One who belongs to the same clan is safe; the semite will never harm his own blood. In the making of a pact, two partners become blood relatives through a juridical fiction. One takes the other into his own personal environment. Pedersen shows that this is emphasized throughout the covenant ceremony. He quotes what Herodotus once wrote about the Bedouins: the covenant partners tear their thumbs and spread the blood evenly on seven stones. Life is in the blood (Lev. 17:11), and its commingling demonstrates community of life.

He describes other practices which bring both partners into complete rapport just as does the blood ritual: one touches the tent rope of his covenant partner, puts on another's articles of dress, wraps the cloak of the other round him. As an example he gives the case of Mohamet, who wraps his cloak round Safijja, thus making her his property. We are immediately tempted to speak about a primitive mentality. What a strange world, we say! And yet this world is not so strange. We know that all people have their peculiar way of life. This includes everything one possesses: home, clothing, tools and all he treasures. A boy who loves his girl respects everything she possesses — her name, her hat, her shawl.

One comes into another's sphere by giving him a hand, a kiss, or by having a meal with him. The

shared meal is a symbol of fraternity. One would
not dine under the Arabic desert tents with an
enemy. Salt also plays a very important role.
Jaussen claims that among nomad tribes it is a
standing law that a host is responsible for his guest
"as long as the salt is still in his stomach" or "lies
on his tongue." He quotes an expression: "Between
this man and that man is salt." This means that the
two are bound by a covenant. A gift has the same
function, according to Pedersen. There are many
symbols by which the partners demonstrate their
unity; to mention one, participation in the same
offering. Pedersen shows the striking similarity between these ceremonies and those of Biblical stories.
He mentions the tale of Jonathan and David. There
was a real soul relationship between Jonathan and
the shepherd of Bethlehem: "Jonathan loved him
as his own soul," says Scripture (1 Sam. 18:1). To
prove this, Jonathan takes off his cloak and gives
it to David. He does the same with his armor, his
sword, his bow and his belt (1 Sam. 18:4). This is
more than a mere donation. If he had desired to
give him a gift, he could have given him new armor,
a new cloak and a new sword. But now he transfers
his own things, and thus lets the other know that he
takes him up into his personal sphere.

Just as among the Arabic tribes, an Israelitic
covenant of one kind or another is often made by a
handshake.

A meal has the same function in Israel. It simultaneously symbolizes and implements a psychic

alliance. This is also our thinking. "The meal," A.
Verheul says, "not only brings people physically, but
also mentally together. To sit at table together in
the fullest sense of the word, where mind and heart
are involved, crystallizes and shows externally what
in reality exists within: they are in harmony and
attuned to one another.[4] Israelites, like the Bedouins,
will never eat and drink with those with whom they
refuse to have community. We read in 1 Kings 13
that Jeroboam made an altar in Bethel; this meant
a schism in the worship of Yahweh. This, in history,
is the great crime of Jeroboam. At the moment when
he went up to the altar to offer, at Yahweh's command, an unknown prophet from Judah came to
reveal the wrath of God. "O, altar, altar!" is the
word of the prophet: "thus says the Lord: Behold,
a son shall be born to the house of David; he shall
sacrifice upon you the priests of the high places who
burn incense upon you, and men's bones shall be
burned upon you!" The king heard these words.
With outstretched hand he cried: "Lay hold of him!"
But the hand which he stretched out against him
withered, so that he could not draw it back. He
submitted to the prophet and begged: "Entreat now
the favor of the Lord your God, and pray for me,
that my hand may be restored to me." The man
of God entreated the Lord; the king's hand was
restored. The king said, "Come home with me, and
refresh yourself, and I will give you a reward," but
the man of God refused. The Lord had forbidden
him: "You shall neither eat bread, nor drink water,
nor return by the way that you came!" The Lord

forbade, because no one is allowed to have community with those who have left him.

Israelites never expected hostility from a table companion. It was a desolating experience for David when he learned that his table companion Achithofel committed treason against him on the occasion of Absalom's revolt. Ps. 41:9 expresses his grief: "Even my bosom friend in whom I trusted, who ate of my bread, has lifted his heel against me." This Scripture statement is also fulfilled in Christ; with a sad heart he must say on the last night of his life: "One of you will betray me" (Jn. 13:21); this too was one of his table companions.

This sign of solidarity is given in Israel by all who make a covenant. Although Isaac has had many disagreeable experiences with Abimelech of Gerar, he agrees to his request for covenant and gives a dinner party. Abimelech, the army lieutenant colonel Phicol and another high functionary are guests who eat and drink (Gen. 26:30). Jacob wishes to forget his quarrels with Laban and to renew his friendship and he gives a dinner party (Gen. 31:46). David also prepares a dinner in honor of Abner (2 Sam. 3:20).

These meals, festive in character, bring the partners together. It might be surprising to hear that salt also played a part in the Israelitic covenants. There could be no successful dinner party without salt to flavor the food. In Num. 18:19 the words of God are directed to the sons and daughters of

Levi: "All the holy offerings which the people of Israel present to the Lord I give to you, and to your sons and daughters with you, as a perpetual due; it is a covenant of salt for ever before the Lord for you and for your offspring with you" — literally an eternal covenant of salt before the countenance of the Lord (cf. 2 Chron. 13:5). Unity in food symbolizes and nourishes community of souls even though it does not actually constitute the community. The emphasis is on the unity. A perfect illustration is Israel's covenant with the Gibeonites: pleasantly impressed by the friendly words of the diplomatic mission from Gibeon, the men of Israel take their food without consulting the Lord (Jos. 9:14). The meal itself is wretched, the bread stale and impalatable. They eat as a gesture of sympathy. By doing so they show their desire for solidarity and thus create a bond of brotherly love.

A gift is also a very important factor in the making of a covenant. It is a demonstration of good will. Accompanied as it is by underlying love — this is always necessary — it is an embodied benevolence. Certain examples show that this is really the case. Abraham accepts the proposal of Abimelech. He is an honest man, and when he takes a part of his flock of sheep and cattle to give to Abimelech, king of Gerar, this is an honest attempt to convince him that he means him well (Gen. 21:27).

In political covenants, where unselfishness is not necessarily the main motivating force, a gift is a means of buying someone's favor. The kings of Israel

and Judah, like many other smaller sovereigns of
the Orient, competed for the favor of powerful
rulers by giving them precious gifts. Hosea reproaches the leaders of the northern state for making
a covenant with Assyria and for bringing oil to Egypt
(12:2). Old monuments still bear witness of this
political ploy. On the black obelisk of Salmanassar
III at the palace of Kalach, a commemorative pillar
picturing great military successes, one can see king
Jehoe, the son of Omri, king of Israel's northern
state: deeply bent to the earth he offers the harsh
Assyrian ruler his fealty. Toward the end of the
eighth century Isaiah, the man of God from the
southern state, laughs at his contemporaries who
put their faith in Egypt. "Everyone comes to shame
through a people that cannot profit them . . . An
oracle on the beasts of the Negeb through a land
of trouble and anguish, from where come the lioness
and the lion, the viper and the flying serpent, they
carry their riches on the backs of asses, and their
treasures on the humps of camels, to a people that
cannot profit them. For Egypt's help is worthless
and empty, therefore I have called her 'Rahab who
sits still'" (Is. 30:5-7). Smaller sovereigns are unwilling to give in to each other; northern and
southern states make covenants and ply each other
with gifts. Toi, ruler of Chamath, happy that the
army of Hadadezer has been defeated by David,
sends his congratulations and gifts of silver, gold
and copper tools (2 Sam. 8:2-10; cf. 1 Kings 15:18-19).
Every one is responsive to a gift; it has been a
popular type of diplomatic persuasion through the

ages. It disarms anger and contributes greatly to
building good relations. The wise men in Israel
knew this (Prov. 21:14) and practiced it. The story
of Nabal and Abigail is well-known: Nabal, the
uncouth, cruel owner of three thousand sheep and
a thousand goats on the steppes of Maon, denied
David and his servants that which they had every
right to expect — a good meal; this was, after all, a
feast. Abigail, a resourceful woman, realized that
revenge was bound to come; she took two hundred
loaves and two skins of wine, five dressed sheep,
five measures of dry grain and two hundred raisin
cakes and two hundred fig cakes; she sent all this
to David and his few hundred men. "And now let
this present which your servant has brought to my
lord be given to the young men who follow my
lord. Pray forgive the trespass of your handmaid,"
is her prayer. David is happy that the crisis is resolved in this way and sends her home in peace
(1 Sam. 25). This disarms anger in the same way
that Jacob pacified Esau with gifts sent ahead by
his servants when he returned from Aram.

Brotherhood as a psychological bond between the
contracting parties is also an important factor in all
covenants. A pact is not merely a juridical entity;
it involves personal commitment. The participants
are made brothers. This word is sometimes explicitly
expressed by those who unite themselves in a covenant or express their desire for one. In his lament
over Jonathan, David calls him "Jonathan, my
brother." This does not appear to be very expressive,
since grief does not weigh words well. We might

offer another example. 1 Kings 20:31-34, narrates that the servants of Ben-ha'dad go to Achab, king of Israel, with sackcloth around their waists and ropes around their necks and say: "Your servant Ben-ha'dad says: Pray, let me live." Achab's answer "Does he still live? He is my brother!" sounds favorable to them and they quickly respond, "Yes, Ben-ha'dad is your brother!" Achab admits him, invites him to come up into his chariot and makes a covenant with him.

This bond is the basis for rights and obligations; in Biblical terminology it is called **chesed.** This is difficult to translate into English. It connotes the benevolence one must feel toward all with whom he is united by blood relationship, friendship, or other tie.

In most cases the covenant partners designate what they expect of each other. However, it might happen that they make an absolute agreement as Jonathan and David do. They oblige themselves to an unlimited benevolence. Such a pact may require that they collaborate in every respect. For this reason Moses often prohibits covenants with the native Canaanites: "Do not make a covenant," Moses says, "with the inhabitants of the country, who play the harlot after their gods. For else they invite you; you eat of their sacrifice; and you take of their daughters for your sons, and their daughters play the harlot after their gods and make your sons play the harlot after their gods (Ex. 34:15; cf. also Ex. 23:32; 34:12; Deut. 7:2).

#### 4. Peace

Where the **chesed** is guaranteed there is peace. This is the serene tranquility of mind possessed when things prosper, when one has everything his heart desires: health and wealth, and everything contributory to happiness. It is a condition of complete inner contentment. It sometimes coincides with what is called salvation. Here in the West we wish our friends the best; Jews and other semites wish peace. Their salutation is the familiar **shalom.** We ask, when we meet a good friend, "How do you do?"; the semite would ask, "Do you have peace?"

One can also speak of **shalom** when mutual relations are good, when they are in accord.

Several times in covenant stories we meet the term "peace." Abimelech asks Isaac to swear not to do him harm, but only to prove affective and let him go in peace, as he did in earlier times; this at least is what he claimed (Gen. 26:29). He desires security, a good relationship that banishes fear. This Isaac promises. What Abimelech desired and obtained, the Gibeonites also obtained. Joshua made peace with them (Jos. 9:15) and this means he made a covenant. For this reason the prophet Abdias can simultaneously speak of "allies" and "men of peace" (Abd. 7).

#### 5. Mutual character of the covenant

In our society the mutual obligations of a covenant are no problem. A covenant is an agreement between equal partners, each of whom undertakes certain responsibilities. This was not always the case in the semitic world. Jonathan is the crown prince; he makes a pact with the shepherd boy David (1 Sam. 18:1-4). David had very little to offer. Nebuchadnezzar appoints a new ruler in Jerusalem, king Sedecias; he makes a covenant with him, "brings him into an **alah**." He must swear fidelity and is not allowed to incite a revolt (Ezek. 17:13-14). Agreement is completely imposed on Sedecias; he can only accept the burdens. This is a unilateral pact because the parties are on entirely different levels — one dictates the terms.

Walter Eichrodt's opinion is that a **berit** always has a mutual character. "Even if the burdens are unequally divided, mutuality is still not excluded."[5] This may be true, but it is often difficult to recognize reciprocity.

In every case the covenant will is present on both sides. We might ask whether David could have rejected Jonathan's gracious offer of a covenant. A comparison might supply an answer. In the East a girl had no choice in the man she married. The young man negotiated with the father. But would she have refused this engagement, if a deeply loved person chose her as the companion of his life? By no means. No one refuses happiness and peace. It is the same with David; otherwise, to quote the words of Gerhard von Rad, "He would have exchanged a valuable relationship, in which one receives protection, against a highly dangerous judicial uncertainty."[6]

When rulers offered a generous covenant, they expected their gracious attitude to be matched by their servant's fidelity and service. In the sovereignty treaties discovered in the near East, we find that oriental potentates speak from a stance of benevolence and require the word of honor from the other party.

## 6. Focus on the covenant of God

Covenant ritual brings the partners together; they belong to one another and are mutually bound by ties of benevolence; they have a guarantee that they will be faithful to one another.

The narratives of God's covenant with Israel are unique. They are relevant for us; and convey a message to us.

According to the Yahwist tradition the Lord called Moses and the heads of Israel to Mount Sinai, where they were allowed to see him — though in a hidden way — and were allowed to eat and drink in his presence; this is equivalent to saying that they were permitted to enter into community with the Lord. The fact that he imposes the ten commandments on them means that he chose them to be his cult-nation.

The Elohist tradition goes further. The people of Israel is not only God's people in that it offers him the required worship; it also lives according to his moral laws. Israel is the nation of the ten commandments, his royal law. God is the great king. The Elohist tradition describes the making of the covenant of Horeb in a manner reminiscent of the oriental sovereigns — persons like Nabuchadnezzar Salmanassar and Assurnirari — made pacts with their vassals. In his highly praised book **The Bible Discovered in Earth and Stone,** G. E. Wright draws our attention to the striking parallelism between the structure of the eastern sovereignty covenants and those of God on Horeb. In these one can distinguish six elements:

1. These agreements always begin with the monarch presenting himself as the great king. It is he who graciously offers the covenant: "Thus says X, the great king . . ." God also begins in the same manner: "I am the Lord, your God . . " (Ex. 20:1-2).

2. Then follows a detailed review of the historical background of the relationships between the great king and the vassal, in which the king's generosity and good deeds occupy the foreground. This is calculated to bind the vassal to the monarch with affectionate ties, making him willingly accept imposed obligations. This God does too: "I am the Lord, your God, who brought you out of the land of Egypt, out of the house of bondage" (Ex. 20:2).

3. After this historical demonstration of the monarch's mercy to vassals has been proved, the definition of the covenant follows, detailing the duties of the vassal. This usually contains a clause in which the vassal is forbidden to enter relationship with foreign powers. God does this in his first commandment, "You shall have no other gods before me."

Laws then follow, in which God explains what he expects of the religious and moral life of his people.

4. The typical sovereignty covenant also prescribed that the charter was to be kept in the sanctuary of the vassal and that at some fixed time, not always clearly defined, public readings of it were to be made . . . This too occurred in Israel. The ten commandments were imprinted on stone tablets (Ex. 24:12) and were to be kept in the sanctuary, in the Ark of the Covenant (Ex. 25:16-21). Periodic reading of the laws to the people is definitely mentioned in Deut. 31:9-13.

5. The fifth significant element was the invocation of the gods of both parties as witnesses of the covenant. In Israel these are missing, or at least not referred to. It is possible, however, that the twelve stones, mentioned in Ex. 24:4 are meant to witness to the covenant. The Bible speaks about similar stones several times. These were customary with the natives of Canaan, and Israel also used them. Jacob set up such a stone at Bethel (Gen. 28:18) after he realized, through the dream of the ladder that reached to heaven, that the place where he had been resting was holy. When he intended to make a covenant with Laban he also set up such a stone. Laban then called this the witness of the covenant (Gen. 31:45, 51, 52). The twelve stones set up by Moses were silent witnesses of everything that happened there: they symbolized the twelve tribes who gave their answer in that place to God's covenant invitation. If one of the two partners does not keep

his word — with the Sinai covenant this is only possible for the human partners, the twelve tribes — the very stones will "start to speak."

6. G. Mendenhall, from whom G. E. Wright took his data, offers a sixth characteristic: the series of blessings and maledictions that will reward or punish those who keep or violate the covenant. These are the only sanctions included, and their implementation is to be made on a purely religious basis. The Book of the Covenant ends with similar blessings and threats (Ex. 23:20-33). The divine king of Israel, after imposing duties on the people, ends with the promises: "Behold, I send an angel before you, to guard you on the way and to bring you to the place which I have prepared. Give heed to him and hearken to his voice, do not rebel against him, for he will not pardon your transgression, for my name is in him. But if you hearken attentively to his voice and do all that I say, then I will be an enemy to your enemies and an adversary to your adversaries. When my angel goes before you, and brings you in to the Amorites, and the Hittites, and the Perizzites, and the Canaanites, the Hivites, and the Jebusites and I blot them out."

When the great king has proclaimed and codified his covenant laws, the people are asked: "Will you accept them?" or "Do you choose me?" God prefers that man make the choice (Ex. 20:20). The people, under the spell of the breakthrough of the divine majesty, accept him and declare themselves willing to keep his commandments. For this reason he makes the covenant with Israel. It is truly bilateral in character.

The ritual, the sprinkling of the altar and the people with the blood of bulls and male goats, shows the unity between God and men. God, represented by the altar, and the people are sprinkled with the same blood and thus communicate in the same life. This unity of life is not merely suggested but it is operative. For this is the power of the blood, that it brings people and things back into the sphere of holiness. "The blood," Lev. 17:11 says, "is only given to you upon the altar to obtain atonement for you, for the blood obtains atonement through the life that is in it." According to the Old Testament, man is drawn into the sphere of unholiness — the power-laden sphere of contamination and evil, the zone of disaster — by sin. Everything that lies within its ambit shares in this contamination. But any person or object signed by the blood of the altar (cf. Ex. 36 ff.) is drawn into the sphere of the holy, of divine favor, and thus is withdrawn from disaster. This makes it understandable why Israel was saved on that historic Easter night in Egypt. The destroyer graciously by-passed their houses, whose doorposts and lintels were covered with blood (Ex. 12:13-23); the blood sanctified them.

The sacrificial blood also sanctified Aaron and his sons (Ex. 29:20-21). Moses, as commanded, sprinkled the blood of the ram on the great toe of the right foot of Aaron and his sons. Literally, they are drawn, from tip to toe, out of the worldly realm. So also the people of Israel, signed with the sacrificial blood, is taken up into the kingdom of God.

God, the great king, adopts Israel as his people. This people has the task of demonstrating God's holiness on this earth. The divine partner will give them a country overflowing with milk and honey.

### 7.  How Israel got its covenant idea

Eastern literature has very little to enlighten us about the covenant idea. It is possible that there were other nations which felt bound by a **berit** with a god; but there is not much evidence of this. In his **La Theologie de l'Ancien Testament I,** P. van Imschoot, cites a few passages showing that Israel is not unique in this regard. According to a Sumerian text, a certain Urakagina, king of Lagas, around 2400 B.C. explains that he received kingship from the god Ningirsu, and that he has passed on to his subjects the word "pronounced by his king Ningirsu." By this "word" he means laws. About 700 B.C. a certain priest-king of the Sabeers performs a cult act, in which he renews the covenant between his god, the king and the people. He submits the countries he conquered to his god and the people, and explains in the name of the national god that he has become **malik** (king) of all South Arabia. The god of Sichem is named, in Judges 9:4, 46, **Baal-Berit.** It is possible that he was honored as a covenant god, because he had made a pact with the sons of Hemor or with the town.

This does not prove the supposition that Israel

called its relationship with God **berit** in imitation of others. It is possible; more cannot be inferred. Even this would argue only an outward similarity. The inner core of Israel's covenant is without parallel in the East, as far as we know.

The God-Israel relationship is a personal one: God in his merciful love chooses a people and asks them to choose him in return. Israel's religion is, as Walter Eichrodt says, **eine Wahlreligion.**[7] The Lord asks Israel to recognize him as the only holy and mighty God; this presumes that they acquiesce to his moral demands. This is a novel request, hitherto unknown in the East. Its religious world was depicted according to an earthly model; there were gods and goddesses; there was no mention of uniqueness, nor of moral holiness. Passions play just as important a role in the world of the gods as they do in the lives of people. If the gods are like this, what can be said of the people? One cannot expect clear water from a troubled spring.

We are familiar with the mythologies of Canaan, where Israel struck her roots. The gods of Canaan are nature gods. Every year, as the myth recreates it, the god Baal, personification of rain and vegetation, is killed in a battle with Mot (death) or with the destroying powers. These powers reign supreme during the season of drought, in the months of May and October. No rain falls then; but in late autumn Baal is again raised to life by his loving, but bellicose, wife Anath or Astoreth. Rainfall returns. The plants grow because Baal was able to mate again with Astoreth, the goddess of fruitfulness. Through them both men and beasts obtain their fertility. "To the Canaanites all blooming and producing of fruit, all begetting and bearing is the activity of the god and the goddess," says Fr. Stier.[8] Canaan celebrated their annual wedding with a sparkling feast of singing and gay music; its own reproductive capacities are being perpetuated. This fertility cult consisted of Canaanite dramatizations of its myths. G. E. Wright says that some of the sexual performances were more than a match for the myths themselves. "The mating of rain and vegetation (of Baal with Astoreth) was obviously imitated on the holy places, under every green tree, by servants of Baal and Astoreth. We know that sacred prostitiution, both male and female, was widespread and was performed in the name of religion in the various centers of worship."[9]

We must investigate the source of Israel's covenant faith. It is obvious that the Hebrews, for whom this pact with God played such an enormous role in its social and cultural life, came to the covenant idea in an original way. The experiences of Israel, starting with the Exodus from Egypt and on Sinai-Horeb, must have deeply impressed them with a consciousness of their alliance with the Lord.

The covenant idea is very ancient; so is its use as an expression of the intimate relationship of man with God. It did not originate in the Deuteronomic period, as some claim.[10] We meet it in the oldest writings of Israel, such as the song of Deborah: "I will make melody, to the Lord God of Israel" (Judges 5:3). It is true that the prophets Amos and Isaiah do not mention a covenant. But they surely have an idea of their inner alliance with God. Amos speaks of the Lord's exceptional care for Israel (3:2), and Isaiah complains about Jerusalem's unfaithfulness: "How the faithful city has become a harlot, she that was full of justice . . ." (1:21). Later he sings the song of the vineyard, in which he praises the love of the Lord for Israel (Is. 5:1-7). God is also the Holy One of Israel (1:4; 4:19, 24; 10:17, 20). He makes Sion his dwelling (Is. 8:18), and this indicates a special involvement. The term **berit** is not used, although the idea of it has already been formulated; Yahwist tradition incorporated it long before Amos, Isaiah and Micah. Did they have a special reason to avoid the term "covenant?" Would its use perhaps have been a hindrance rather than a help? The people could interpret it in terms of offering gifts and sacrifice without including a moral attitude toward life. This is the explanation given by the Catholic exegetes, P. V. Imschoot and V. Hamp.[11] This may be a valid reason; it is a fact that these prophets repeatedly insist that the people follow moral norms: "Seek good, and not evil; that you may live," is the watchword of Amos (5:14). And Isaiah says to the scoffers in Jerusalem, who think they are secure because they claimed they had made a covenant with death: "therefore thus says the Lord God: Behold, I am laying in Zion for a foundation a stone, a tested stone, a precious cornerstone, of a sure foundation. He who believes will not be in haste. And I will make justice the line, and righteousness the plummet" (Is. 28:16, 17). The message of these prophets attempts to elevate moral life. They were unable to appeal to the covenant; Amos and Isaiah preached in the Southern state where the idea that the God of the covenant makes moral demands had not yet penetrated. The Yahwist covenant tradition demands worship from the human partners. Moral laws are not mentioned. Therefore, reference to the covenant would have been useless in the Southern state in those days.

# 2

# DEVELOPMENT OF THE
# COVENANT IDEA

On Mount Sinai-Horeb Israel became conscious that it is God's People. This was a first principle, a concept on which they based their lives, a starting point for further reflection, as is Jesus' death and resurrection for our theologians. The Spirit of God testified to it. The Lord raised up men whose duty it was to keep the people in the bond of his love, and especially to urge them to be faithful to their word.

## 1. Hosea

When Hosea appears in the middle of the eighth century, it is he who first enriched our knowledge of the relationship between God and Israel with the image of the marriage union. God is the bride-groom, Israel the bride. This is a realistic comparison. Our first impression, however, might be that it does not adequately portray the immense distance between God and man. But if we conclude this we are thinking of marriage in western culture. In Old Testament days the groom had to buy his bride (Ex. 22:16; Deut. 22:29). He was engaged to her (Gen. 24:49 ff.).

She became his property and was — we put this crudely — his chattel as was his mule or ox. Exodus lists the woman along with the ox and the mule as one of the properties of the neighbor which may not be coveted, according to the tenth of the Hebrew commandments (Ex. 20:17). The husband could do with her as he wished: he was her **baal,** her lord. He could divorce her, though she obviously could not divorce him. Thus in the East wedlock was primarily a legalistic contract alliance. This does not mean of course that the relationship between man and woman in every case was as cold as the money he spent on her. She was not merely a thing on which he could divert himself. One who buys something, does so because he desires it. The love of a man for a woman was probably just as emotional as it is in our time: it is the man, as Gen. 2:24 says, who leaves father and mother to attach himself to the woman. But her juridical position is different: she is placed at the husband's disposal; she is meant for man, and therefore her function is to surrender herself completely to him, to obey him absolutely. She is not allowed to have anyone beside him; the man is the jealous partner.

Hosea used this as his first image, arrived at it through his experiences in his own love-life. A disciple tells about his troubles: "The Lord spoke to Hosea, Go, take an adulterous woman and have bastard children with her; for the country committed adultery and turned away from the Lord. Therefore he married Gomer, daughter of Diblaim; she became pregnant and gave birth to a son."

Hosea gave his children symbolic names, as Isaiah was to do later. He named his first son "Jezreel," because the Lord will punish the royal house which had established its government in Jezreel. The second child, a girl, is named "Without-pity"; the Lord intends to support the people no longer: he is to hand it over ruthlessly to the enemies of the people. The third child is a boy; his name "Not-my-people" is again an indication that God withdraws as protector and father.

This story presents a real difficulty: Did God really demand this of him? Is this not inhuman? Did Hosea have to take a woman whom he knows beforehand will be unfaithful to him? Did he really love her?

It is not easy to reconstruct the actual facts. But let us not forget that this is a prophet talking. When we read of the vocation of Isaiah and hear the order of the Lord: "Make the heart of this people fat, and their ears heavy, and shut their eyes; lest they see with their eyes, and hear with their ears, and understand with their hearts and turn and be healed" (Is. 6:10), we face the same problem. Does God really want people to perish? No. Nor does he want them to be blinded. In fact, he sent the prophet to accomplish the opposite. But because the people in fact were stubborn and indifferent, Isaiah speaks as if he has received orders to harden them. The message assumes a different aspect and the prophet's disillusionment takes on a new dimension. This is the key to the story of Hosea. We can

confidently say that he really loved Gomer: she was
the girl of his heart. He married her with the best
of expectations, but he is to be bitterly disappointed.
Then he comes to see everything that happened as
a divine plan and as a symbol of everything God
endured with Israel. He narrates the story of Gomer's
unfaithfulness from the point of view of this prophetic
vision; his own difficulties are an image of God's
experience. Just as he grieved over Gomer's unfaithfulness, God is disappointed with Israel's lapses.
Therefore his words are harsh: "Plead with your
mother, plead — for she is not my wife and I am not
her husband — that she put away her harlotry from
her face, and her adultery from between her breasts"
(Hos. 2:4). You are not my wife anymore; I am no
longer your husband. Here the Lord also pronounces
his divorce. His word given at the wedding ceremony — at the making of the covenant on the
Sinai — is now nullified. His once-promised faithfulness is withdrawn from the people. But, this is
not an irrevocable dismissal; God leaves the door
open to a renewed experience of matrimonial love.
The Lord's love, **chesed,** challenges his bride's unfaithfulness! He speaks about the time when she
will return to her husband, and both will experience
a second honeymoon, just like the one they knew in
the happy days of their wandering in the desert
(Hos. 2:13-14). As Jeremiah later (2:2-3) idealizes
the time in the desert, we note that Hosea pictures
it as a period when Israel was completely content
with the Lord and felt safe only with him.

In chapter 3 Hosea relates that the Lord again orders him to love a woman who pursues other men. Literally it says: "Go again, love a woman who is beloved of a paramour and is an adulteress; even as the Lord loves the people of Israel, though they turn to other gods and love cakes of raisins. So I bought her for fifteen shekels of silver and a homer and a half of barley. And I said to her, you shall not play the harlot, or belong to another man; so will I also be to you. For the children of Israel shall dwell many days without king or prince, without sacrifice or pillar, without ephod or teraphim" (3:1-4). The common interpretation is that Hosea must win back his wife. There are objections however, for it is written: love "a woman . . .," not "your wife." Besides, it would be very strange if a person had to pay again for his divorced wife. There is a law that says that one is not allowed to bring back his runaway wife. The solution of this difficulty is not easy. Could it be possible that Hosea must begin anew a love adventure with a woman who has a bad name? Could this possibly be an indication of the fact that the Lord himself, time after time, again witnesses his love for Israel? What Hosea demands of her is obviously that she be denied the pleasure of matrimonial cohabitation for a time. This indicates what Israel must undergo, namely, that she will, for a notable period, be without a king, without sacrifices. She will go into exile.

Israel's infidelity is seen in terms of the covenant: 6:7 says: "They transgressed my covenant, and they

dealt faithlessly with me." "Covenant" here means
the Law and the transgressions are seen within its
context. The law is so closely related to the covenant
that both are frequently mentioned in the same
breath. Thus Hos. 8:1: "Set the trumpet to your
lips, for a vulture is over the house of the Lord,
because they have broken my covenant, and transgressed my law."

The picture of Israel as bride of the Lord returns
in later Old Testament writings: Deut. 31:16; Jer.
3:4; 3:6-11; Ps. 73:27; and in Ezek. 16; each time it
concerns the unfaithfulness of Israel. For the moment
we are concerned with the merciful love of God,
who wraps a close bond around his adopted people.
Then we see how beautifully Ezekiel compliments
Hosea.

Ezekiel recounts the history of the Lord's love and
Israel's infidelity in chapter 16. We cannot say much
good about Israel's origin; she, (Jerusalem) is the
fruit of an Amoritic father and a Hittite mother.
When she was born, there was no loving mother to
take care of her. She was abandoned, she was
doomed to perish. The Lord passed by, saw her
struggling in her blood and took pity on her. He
kept her alive. This is the Lord's first loving act.
Without a doubt the covenant with Abraham is
indicated here. She grows up, becomes a beautiful
girl. The years of love begin. The Lord sees that
she is still naked: this is the symbol of the poor and
miserable situation of the people in Egypt. He
wraps his cloak around her and covers her shame

— a well known gesture of protection and matrimonial unity. (Compare Ruth 3:9). The Lord swears faithfulness to her and makes a covenant with her and thus she belongs to him (16:8). He dresses her in gay clothes, gives her shoes, wraps her in fine silks and decorates her with jewelry, bracelets and ribbons. He makes a royal bride of her (16:10-14). Then the prophet narrates a seeming impossibility: this bride, having everything a woman in the East could desire, throws herself away as a prostitute. Money does not matter to her, for she possesses everything; she even offers her lovers gifts. But lust is important to her. She is a harlot (16:35 and others).

**Israel: Son of God.** Hosea first refers to Israel's infidelity as the bride; later (chap. 11) he speaks about the self-centeredness of the son adopted by God. In 11:1 we read: "When Israel was a child, I loved him, and out of Egypt I called my son." This is similar to Ex. 4:22: "Israel is my first-born son, thus says the Lord." Hosea describes Israel as the son who shuts his eyes to all which his father did for him. The Lord taught Ephraim, one of Israel's tribes, to make its first steps, even carried it. He bound it to himself with bonds of love and pity (11:2, 3). When there is no response to that love, he orders Hosea to say that it will be turned over to Egypt; Egypt here is the symbol of Assyria (11:5). The relationship between God and Israel is that of father and son. This appears again in Deut. 32:6, 18; Jer. 3:14, 19; 31:9; Is. 63:16; 64:8; Mal. 1:6; 2:10; 1 Chron. 29:10.

Israel is the **prototokos** (first-born), says Esdras (4:22) and Jeremiah (31:9). This is a favored position in Jewish families as we can see from the synonym **ben jaqqir,** that is, "mother's darling" (cf. Jer. 31:20).

The implications of the word "father" are varied; When referring to God it does not connote physical reproduction as far as the Israelites are concerned. It rather points to the special way in which a group became his people. Deut. 32:6 notes three elements: "Is he not your father, who created you, who made you and established you?" These explain each other. God made the people (Is. 43:15 says "created"), he adopted it at birth, he acquired it by purchasing it from the pharaoh. Consequently, he is father because he has given existence to the people and surrounded it with special care.

**Israel: the vine.** The vine is from time immemorial the symbol of a vitality capable of limitless development. The prophet Hosea first makes use of this image when he notes that Israel has failed to produce the fruits one might expect from a vine (Hos. 10:1). Isaiah develops this metaphor further by speaking of the vineyard of the Lord and God's care for it. "My friend had a vineyard on a very fertile hill. He digged it and cleared it of stones, and planted it with choice vines; he built a watch tower in the midst of it, and hewed out a wine vat in it; and he looked for it to yield grapes, but it yielded wild grapes" (Is. 5:1, 2). What could his friend do? He has a right to be angry. "I will remove its hedge, and it shall be devoured; I will break down its wall and it shall be trampled down. I will make it a waste; it shall not be pruned or hoed, and briers and thorns shall grow up; I will also command the clouds that they rain no rain upon it" (5:5, 6).

Jeremiah remembers this image a century later. He too complains: "Yet I planted you a choice vine, wholly of pure seed. How then have you turned degenerate and become a wild vine?" (Jer. 2:21; cf. 12:10).

Israel's infidelity was the basis for representing the relationship of God to Israel under new images: God is the groom, Israel the bride; God is the father, Israel the son; God is the vintager, Israel the vine.

## 2. Deuteronomy

The theological reflection of the prophets is portrayed in two other editions of the Mosaic covenant: in Deuteronomy and in the priestly codex.

Deuteronomy, written about 700, introduces a new Law-experience into the spirit of Moses. It implies how the people of the time regarded its relationship with God.

Like Hosea, it occasionally speaks of the covenant as the ten commandments because of the great psychological influence the decalog had on covenant observance. References to violating or ordering of the covenant are examples (Deut. 4:10; 4:14; 17:1; Jos. 7:11; 23:6; Judg. 2:20 etc.). This is not unusual; The way the covenant relationship is characterized is more important.

In the Yahwist and Elohist tradition this union was represented in a covenant ceremony. Deuteronomy's description clearly reminds us of the marriage ceremony. When the Lord, through Moses, presented his "Second Law" to the people in the land of Moab — a law relevant to the new situation Israel will face in Canaan — Moses says: "this day the Lord your God commands you to fulfill these statutes and ordinances; you shall therefore be careful to maintain them with all your heart and with all your soul. You have declared this day concerning the Lord that he is your God . . . and the Lord has declared this day concerning you that you are a people for his own possession, as he has promised you, and that you are to keep all his commandments, that he will set you high above all nations that he has made, in praise and in fame and in honor, and that you shall be a people holy to the Lord your God, as he has spoken" (Deut. 26:17-19). Moses says the same in his last speech where he encourages the people to be faithful: "You stand this day all of you before the Lord your God, the heads of your tribes, your elders, and your officers, all the men of Israel, your little ones, your wives, and the sojourners who are in your camp, both he who hews your wood and he who draws your water, that you may enter into the solemn oath (**Alah,** the oath through which one calls away God's punishment), of the Lord your God, which the Lord your God makes with you this day, that he may establish you this day as his people, and that he may be your God, as he promised you, and as he swore to your fathers, to Abraham, to Isaac, and to Jacob" (Deut. 29:9-12).

Another typical Deuteronomic formula is: "You will be my own possession" (Deut. 26:18; 7:6; 14:2 and in Ex. 19:5). The latter text is so typically Deuteronomic that it must originate from that source. Compare Deut. 32:11 with its eagle-image and Ex. 19:4. The Hebrew term is **segullah** which means "personal possession." David says that he will give part of his private property for the building of the temple (1 Chron. 29:3). The term appears elsewhere only in Ps. 135:4; 1 Chron. 29:3; Eccl. 2:8; and Mal. 3:17. Israel is the private property of the Lord; this is an exclusive title, for if it is true that the heart is where the treasure is (cf. Mt. 6:19), then the Lord loves Israel. This involves obligations on the part of the people; it is allowed to give its heart only to the Lord (cf. Deut. 26:17-19).

Israel is the segullah of the Lord; this is also expressed in the formula, Israel is the heritage **(nachalah)** of the Lord. The redemption of the people from Egypt should have made Israel the heritage of the Lord. "The Lord has taken you, and brought you forth out of the iron furnace, out of Egypt, to be a people of his own possession, as at this day" (Deut. 4:20). In the song of Moses, the hymn of the Lord's loving care for Israel, the poet recalls former days. "When the Most High gave to the nations their inheritance, (which means: to every nation its land) when he separated the sons of men, he fixed the bounds of the peoples according

to the number of the sons of Israel" (Deut. 32:8).
This Hebrew text has never been understood properly. The Greek translation has: "According to the
sons of God" which might mean that God divides
the earth according to the number of his angels. This
is an opinion which was common in Jewish society
about 200 B.C. Daniel says that every nation has
its own protecting angel. The Greek translation
then continues: "And the Lord's portion was his
people, Jacob his allotted heritage" (Deut. 32:9).
The Lord kept the people of Israel as his own. This
is a meaningful simile to express his preference for
Israel. Deuteronomy continues: "He found him in
desert land, and in the howling waste of the wilderness; he encircled him, he cared for him, he kept
him as the apple of his eye. Like an eagle that
stirs up its nest, that flutters over its young, spread-
ing out its wings, catching them, bearing them,
bearing them on its pinions" (Deut. 32:10-11).

Human beings cherish their heritage with rever-
ential love. When God's anger looms threateningly
we find the leaders of Israel reminding him that he
has accepted their land as his heritage. Moses tells
how he prostrated himself before the Lord when he
threatened to destroy the people. He prayed: "O
Lord God, destroy not thy people and thy heritage,
whom thou hast redeemed through thy greatness,
whom thou hast brought out of Egypt with a
mighty hand" (Deut. 9:25, 26). Solomon throws
himself on the Lord's mercy with regard to his
heritage: "Forgive thy people . . ., for they are thy

people, and thy heritage, which thou didst bring out of Egypt, from the midst of the iron furnace" (1 Kings 8:51). In the literature of Israel the people are usually the heritage: 1 Sam. 10:1; 26:19; 2 Sam. 15:16; 20:19; 21:3; Is. 19:25; 47:6; Joel 4:2; 2:17; Ps. 78:71; 79:1-5; Jer. 12:9; (in Jeremiah however the country of Canaan is the heritage in most texts), Jer. 2:7; 3:19; 12:14; 16:18; 50:11. Since country and people are inseparable, this difference is inconsequential.

**Holy people:** Sprinkling with sacrificial blood symbolized and caused (remission of sins and took the people back into the sphere of God. They are again holy. The Deuteronomic tradition is explicit: 7:6; 14:2; 26:19 and 28:9.

Who is holy? God! Everything upon which God lays his hand is holy. God himself is the thrice holy (cf. Is. 6:3-5) and all creation trembles before him. Objects which God sets apart like Mount Sinai are also holy: no one is allowed near it, unless he is sanctified; therefore Sinai is reserved. The vicinity of the burning bush is holy ground, where people must remove their shoes. The temple of Jerusalem is holy, although not to the same extent throughout: God himself resides in the Holy of Holies and the high priest alone is allowed to enter once a year and then only with the blood of atonement. Jerusalem shares in its holiness, as do the Ark of Covenant, the altar and its ministers. Finally, the people are holy because the Lord has chosen them to be his own possession and his heritage.

**The chosen people:** At any marriage one might ask why did this woman marry this man? The answer without a doubt would be that he loves her. When she has found her place as a respected woman because of him, his was a "graceful" choice.

Israel is the bride of the Lord, his possession, his heritage, his holy people. Deuteronomy gives the reason: "The Lord your God has chosen you to be a people for his own possession, out of all the peoples that are on the face of the earth" (Deut. 7:6). The solemn covenant is made on Sinai. But long before God had already made his choice and prepared this "marriage." Exactly when he began to set Israel apart, is difficult to say. The prophets Amos, Hosea, Isaiah, Micah, speak only about the election of Israel as a people. Deuteronomy places this election and covenant in the era of the patriarchs: "And because he loved your fathers and chose their descendants after them, and brought you out of Egypt in person with his great power . . ." (Deut. 4:37; cf. 10:15). The source of this choice is his love. This is not because they are lovable people; there is therefore no reason for them to take a haughty attitude toward others. Against their inclination to boast of their exceptional position among the peoples — a presumption Paul also encountered (cf. Rom. 2-4) — Moses points to its gratuitous character. Israel does not at all deserve its vocation. He says, "It was not because you were more numerous than any other people that the Lord set his love upon you and chose you, for you were the fewest of all peoples; but it is because the Lord loves you, and is keeping the oath which he swore to your fathers, that the Lord has brought you out with a mighty hand, and redeemed you from the house of bondage, from the hand of Pharaoh, king of Egypt" (Deut. 7:7-8). To others who assume a self-satisfied attitude he says, "Not because of your righteousness or the uprightness of your heart are you going in to possess their land; but because of the wickedness of these nations the Lord your God is driving them out from before you, that he may confirm the word which the Lord swore to your fathers, to Abraham, to Isaac, and to Jacob" (Deut. 9:5). Israel itself cannot demand distinction. It has received everything only because of God's inscrutable mercy. Election is not to be construed as a license to sin. There are no privileges for the Israelites, nor will God overlook their iniquities. The prophet Amos convinces them of this: "You only have I known of all the families of the earth; therefore I will punish you for all your iniquities" (3:2). From those to whom much is given, much is expected. Moses points to punishments of the past; "Your eyes have seen what the Lord did at Baal — Peor; for the Lord your God destroyed from among all the men who followed the Baal of Peor; but you who held fast to the Lord your God are all alive this day" (Deut. 4:3-4). God's **chesed** calls for the fulfillment of the commandment: "and you shall love the Lord your God with all your heart, and with all your soul, and with all your might" (Deut. 6:5). They must keep the commandments and the regulations and then, "The Lord your God will keep with you the covenant and the steadfast love which he swore to your fathers to keep" (Deut. 7:12).

Thus the covenant in the Deuteronomic setting is depicted as a fruit of the Lord's mercy and faithfulness to his word (cf. Deut. 7:8).

While the old prophets Hosea, Amos, Isaiah and Micah do not mention the promises made to the fathers, the Mosaic traditions refer to Israel's historical position among nations, and to the origins of its people's existence. Deuteronomy presents this in a positive way; in the tradition of the priestly writers the covenant with Abraham dominates the history of Israel. This depends on the ever growing spiritualization of the image of God.

### 3.  The priestly tradition

The image of God formed by the priestly editors in and after the Babylonian exile (587-539) is more transcendentally superhuman than ever before. This is graphically illustrated by the creation story on the first page of Genesis. God summons his creatures, and they come: "Let there be light, and there was light." His word is not empty; it is productive. No word returns unfilled to this speaker. The God of this tradition is he who gives life and fruitfulness to all creatures, humans and animals: "Be fruitful and multiply." In this priestly perspective the seventh day is holy: "God rested the seventh day." It can be seen that God is still spoken of in a human way. A typical expression for holiness is used for the first time in the short sketch of the life of Henoch: ". . . and he walked with God" (Gen. 5:24).

This development of the concept of God and the holiness ideal have had an influence on covenant traditions.

a. It influenced the mode of expression. While the old writings use common terminology, the well-known **karat berit** (cutting the covenant), the priestly writings say, that God **gives** his covenant (Gen. 9:12; 17:2; Num. 25:12). They abandon anthropomorphic description and accentuate the merciful character of the pact. Or they speak about "establishing a covenant" (Gen. 6:18; 9:9 ff.; 17:7; etc.) which emphasizes its durability. Frequently its enduring character is further strengthened by the term "eternal," as used in Gen. 9:16; 17:7, 13, 19; Ex. 31:16; Lev. 24:8.

b. It also influenced covenant history. Because God's word is effective and his assurance never fails, the priestly tradition recognizes only one covenant which establishes a relationship between God and Israel, namely that made with Abraham. The Sinai pact is only a realization and an expansion of the one made with the patriarchs.

c. It further influenced the covenant idea: The eternal pact remains, even if the people deviate from it. God's promise always endures. When people leave him, fulfillment of the promise is only suspended. Lev. 26:41 says, "If then their uncircumcised heart is humbled and they make amends for their iniquity, then I will remember my covenant with Jacob, and I will remember my covenant with Isaac and my covenant with Abraham, and I will remember the land. But the land shall be left by them, and enjoy its sabbaths while it lies desolate without them; and they shall make amends for their iniquity, because they spurned my ordinances, and their soul abhorred my statutes. Yet for all that, when they are in the land of their enemies, I will not spurn them, neither will I abhor them so as to destroy them utterly and break my covenant with them, for I am the Lord their God." The covenant as such does not depend on human cooperation for its rise or fall.

This is illustrated by the covenant stories. In the agreement with Noah, mentioned only in the priestly writings, God says: "I establish my covenant with you, that never again shall all flesh be cut off by the waters of a flood, and never again shall there be a flood to destroy the earth" (Gen. 9:11). This is an assurance, given to the survivors, that henceforth they may live in security. They will be able to execute God's order to populate the earth. Not only human beings, but the whole earth is assured that it will never again be abandoned to destruction. God makes this agreement with Noah, the representative of the people, because he is a righteous and blameless man who corresponds to the holiness ideal: He walked with God (Gen. 6:9).

A typical characteristic of this tradition is that God always gives a sign. In Noah's covenant it is the rainbow. "I set my bow in the cloud, and it shall be a sign of the covenant between me and the earth. When I bring clouds over the earth and the bow is seen in the clouds, I will remember my covenant which is between me and you and every living creature of all flesh; and the waters shall

never again become a flood to destroy all flesh"
(Gen. 9:13-15).

The compact with Abraham is the fundamental
one. The narrative opens with an introduction in
which God announces his plan: "I am God Almighty;
walk before me, and be blameless. And I will make
my covenant between me and you, and will multiply
you exceedingly" (Gen. 17:1-2).

Then he elaborates: "I will make you the father
of a multitude of nations. I will make you exceedingly fruitful; and I will make nations of you, and
kings shall come forth from you. I will establish
my covenant between you and me and your descendants after you throughout their generations, as a
perpetual covenant, that I may be a God to you
and to your descendants after you. And I will give
to you, and to your descendants after you, the land
of your sojournings, all the land of Canaan, for an
everlasting possession; and I will be their God"
(Gen. 17:5-8). Finally he enumerates the obligations
which bind Abraham. He must circumcise every
male child when it is eight days old. That is a
necessary condition: no one may participate in worship if he is not circumcised (cf. Ex. 12:48). This
ancient initiation ritual here receives a theological
meaning; it becomes a sign that one belongs to the
covenant people. During the exile this became a dis-
tinguishing mark of great importance and was therefore made obligatory. It helped the people of Israel
to keep their identity in foreign lands.

This covenant with Abraham has dynamic power.

As the seed bursts open in a field moistened by rain, so does this word. Subsequent history clearly unfolded under its aegis. The priestly tradition shows how God realized the promises given to Abraham, how his descendants become numerous and how God delivers this people from the oppression of their Egyptian overlords, and makes them his people.

When Israel sighs under hard labor in Egypt, God appears and says to Moses, "I am the Lord. I appeared to Abraham, to Isaac and to Jacob, as God Almighty, but by my name the Lord I did not make myself known to them. I also established my covenant with them, to give them the land of Canaan, the land in which they dwelt as sojourners. Moreover I have heard the groaning of the people of Israel whom the Egyptians hold in bondage and I have remembered my covenant" (Ex. 6:2-3).

God promises a special relationship between himself and Abraham's descendants: "Their God I will be." This intimacy, which bears the character of a matrimonial alliance, is realized, or will be realized when the Lord redeems the people from Egypt. In Ex. 6:4-5 God indicates that he will establish this fairly soon. He says, "I will bring you out from under the burdens of the Egyptians, and I will deliver you from their bondage, and I will redeem you." "To redeem" is **gaal** in Hebrew; it means to buy off or to claim with the basic underlying thought of protection. This concept has a special connotation. When a member of a family wishes to sell

a part of the land, other members of the families
concerned are obliged to make sure that this property
will not be lost to the family. This is an expression
of the ancestral solidarity of the East. When some
other member bought this strip of land — other goods
might fall under the same heading — then he was
the "unloader" (goel), (cf. Ruth 3:12; 4:1-12). When
God promises to redeem his people, this is an act
of kindness or redemption. It might be better to
say that God stands up for his people. Here again
the graciousness of the covenant appears: "Fear not,
for I have redeemed you (gaal); I have called you
by name, you are mine" (Is. 43:1). In Ex. 6:6-8 the
Lord gives his people confidence by his word and
promise that he will treat it like a bride: "I will be
your God; and you shall know that I am the Lord
your God, who has brought you out from under the
burdens of the Egyptians. And I will bring you into
the land which I swore to give to Abraham, to Isaac,
and to Jacob; I will give it to you for a possession, I
am the Lord." Israel feels safe; the Lord will take
her as his bride into his land.

The Sinai covenant is the fulfillment of the one
made with Abraham; this (Sinai) is not the foundation of God's gracious operation. If it were, we
would have difficulty in interpreting the solemn
closing expression (Ausklang) of the holiness law
where Yahweh promises that if the people will make
amends for their iniquity he will remember his
covenant with Jacob and with Isaac and with
Abraham (Lev. 26:42). On Sinai no new promise

came from God. What he gave there, according to these traditions — instructions, institutions and laws, was an adjustment of his pact with Abraham due to a changed situation.

But again he gives a sign. As he gave Abraham the sign of circumcision, on Sinai he gives the celebration of the Sabbath: "The Sabbath," in God's words, "is a sign between me and you throughout your generations, that you may know that I, the Lord, sanctify you" (Ex. 31:13). Through the keeping of the commandments the people will be, as Ex. 19:6 says, a kingdom of priests and a holy nation.

No matter how the attitude of the Lord is represented, whether of king to vassal (Elohistic tradition), of a groom to bride, of father to son, of vine-dresser to vine or vineyard (Hosea), the covenant is always the sign of God's election. He mercifully takes Israel into his sphere of influence. Likewise, a decision is always demanded from the people. This is totalitarian in the sense that Israel must measure up to the ideal picture that God himself has made of his bride: he insists on one, "who is without spot or wrinkle or any such thing" (cf. Eph. 5:27).

Because the merciful initiative is always from God, the Greek translation, the Septuagint, usually renders the Hebrew **berit** with the Greek **diatèkè**. This word seldom means covenant, but rather a special, free disposition, a last will. Translators use this word, even when it clearly designates a covenant, as in Gen. 21:27 and Is. 28:18. This Greek translation is the origin of our use of the word "testament" instead of "covenant." This translation conveys the idea of the merciful initiative of God very well, but does not emphasize the human response created by God's act.

## 4. Judaism

The exile purified Israel. It accomplished what ages of prophetic preaching were unable to achieve: faithfulness to Yahweh and to his Law.

The Law became the highest authority in the last four centuries before Christ. God's Law lives in Israel and Israel lives in the Law. Throughout the psalms of that period a joyous theme of love for the Law resounds (Ps. 1; 19:8-11; 119). It is written in Israel's heart but it still does not know Yahweh as he is.

We have already noted that in the Deuteronomic writings the Law on which the covenant is based, soon comes to be called the covenant. That trend continues: 2 Chron. 6:11; Sir. 24:23; 1 Macc. 1:57; 2:27, 50 etc. Studying of the Law becomes the core of Jewish religion in the last few centuries before Christ. Jewish religion and the society in which it lives is eventually identified with covenant. This is shown in the book of Daniel. The author, speaking about Antiochus IV the anti-Christ of his time, says that he will return to his country with evil designs against the holy covenant (11:28) and that he will act against it (11:30). Without a doubt this refers to Jewish society united to God in a holy pact (cf. 1 Macc. 1:15).

During this period, the Law was given such prominence that the Jewish people actually overlooked the Lord who was its creator and who had taken them up into communion with himself. At least certain groups develop the idea that they are saving themselves and they present themselves before God, hands open to receive the wages of their good works. To give an example, they expressed this in their interpretation of Abraham's history. They considered his election not purely as a divine gift, but as a recompense. Some rabbinic circles described Abraham as the one who discovered monotheism in his native country and abandoned the gods of his fathers. Therefore Nimrod had him thrown into an iron furnace. But God saved him. Abraham, Isaac and Jacob obeyed all the laws; they accumulated an inexhaustible fund of merits, and on the basis of these God redeemed the people from Egypt. Some authors even claimed that membership in the family of Abraham was a guarantee of salvation. John the Baptist tries to undermine this Jewish self-sufficiency when he prepares the hearts of the people for the coming kingdom of the Lord: "Do not begin to say to yourselves, we have Abraham as our father; for I tell you, God is able from these stones to raise up children to Abraham" (Lk. 3:8). This explains the significant difference between the Biblical and the later Jewish concept of the covenant.

Rabbis seldom discussed the Biblical concept that man is not on the same level with God. They prefer to speak about the covenant and to swear

by it. The Israelites are called the sons of the covenant: their proselytes enter into it. They are proud
of its signs, circumcision and the sabbath until it
gradually comes to be identified with them. It becomes a glorious title, like descent from Abraham,
on which they rely in claiming favors from God.

The Lord's choice of this people resulted in a
special relationship of love between God and Israel,
noted in such expressions as, "The Lord God of
Israel" — "the people," "people of God." This concept is mentioned by apocryphal writers but not
by the rabbis. They preferred to speak about the
mutual love between God and Israel, rather than
about the primacy of God's love. They referred to
the people by using the characteristic **am segullah**
(the Lord's own property). Here again national pride
is seen. Their pretentious assertion is worse: "One
Israelite is worth more than all nations of the earth."
They feel they are intimate friends of God, dearly-
beloved-ones, loved by him as the pupil of his eye,
his true sons. They prefer this image to the image
of the bride, showing their inclination to heighten
the human contribution in relation to God. They
consider the image of bridal relationship as less
appropriate.

Before discussing the New Testament, a word
about Israel's response to the covenant gift of the
Lord might be fitting. In the light of the reaction of
the chosen people we can readily see the need for
renewal of the pact.

# 3

# THE RESPONSE OF ISRAEL

There are numerous aspects of Israel's response to the covenant which offer themselves for consideration. We might focus attention on the heart-warming reaction of truly religious individuals who promptly expressed their adherence to God. Or, contrariwise, we might point to the unfaithful ones, already mentioned by Hosea and Ezekiel. We prefer to begin on the brighter side; this is more in keeping with what we have seen in the preceding chapter where we saw the Lord addressing his people as "my people, my bride, my precious possession." Hence we emphasize first the faithful reaction of the bride.

## 1. In Yahweh's haven of salvation

The covenant relationship gives peace because one party derives security and trust from the other; he feels safe in a harbor. With the assurance of salvation from Yahweh, Israel depends on him and feels secure in him. Expressions of this confidence are widened in prayer literature. This often relates how the religious person takes refuge in the Lord in all his successes and reverses: "Preserve me, O God, for in thee I take refuge. I say to the Lord: Thou art my Lord; I have no good apart from thee" (Ps. 16:1, 2).

the echo of its belief. But the sincere faith of a committed man is in violent contrast to the unfaithfulness of the people as a whole.

## 2.   They have turned their backs on me

Where the ground is rocky, seed develops with surprising speed. But when the sun burns down on the young plant, it shrivels just as quickly. The rocky soil prevents development of roots and absorption of moisture. We are reminded of this statement of Christ (Mt. 13:5) when we hear, in the covenant story in Ex. 24:3-8, how eagerly the people of Israel accept the conditions of the Lord — and then dance around the golden calf on Sinai before forty days have passed. "Make us gods, who shall go before us," they tell Aaron, "as for this Moses, the man who brought us up out of the land of Egypt, we do not know what has become of him." Aaron cannot resist the people. He asks for the gold earrings of the women, sons and daughters, and makes a molten calf. The people cry, "These are your gods, who brought you up out of the land of Egypt." But Yahweh, the God of the heavens, does not allow himself to be misrepresented. He already had absolutely prohibited this sort of thing. This however had not penetrated the minds of the people: they were slow to understand; the Lord himself called them "stiff-necked" (Ex. 32:9). If Moses had not stood in the breach for them, God would have rejected them right there.

Their dance around the calf symbolized the ficklemindedness of this people.

But this is only the beginning. In the land of Canaan a still greater temptation is awaiting them: they are exposed to a worship which appeals more to their base passions than does the spiritualized cult of Yahweh. The sons of Israel are fascinated by the frenzied ritual of the native religious practices. Their worship on the high places with its unrestrained agricultural mimes, their temples filled and surrounded by female and male prostitutes, had a great attraction for the nomadic people.

They exchange Yahweh for the baals and the Astoreth (cf. Judg. 2:11-13). From other texts we learn that they still retain the Lord, but that they do not understand his real nature. This is obvious in their worship. They treat God as if he were one of the baals. This is the meaning of the hope: "On that day it will be: she will call me my husband and not my baal anymore!" It is probable that some of the people actually transferred the sensual worship of Baal and Astoreth to the Lord, for we read in Deut. 23:18-19: "There shall be no cult prostitute among the daughters of Israel, neither shall there be a cult prostitute among the sons of Israel: You shall not bring the hire of a harlot, or the wages of a male prostitute into the house of the Lord your God in payment of any vow (that is, to serve as a gift to God as substitute for some other promise); for both of these are an abomination to the Lord your God" (cf. also 1 Kings 14:23, 24; 2 Kings 23:7).

Heathen cult panders to the human tendency to exhibitionism. People offer their children for sacri-

speedily! Be thou a rock of refuge for me, a strong fortress to save me! Yea, thou art my rock and my fortress; for thy name's sake" (3:4) (cf. Ps. 19:5; 28:1; 62:3; 62:7, 8; 73:26; 78:35; 89:27; 91:12; 94:22; 95:1; 144:1). The meaning is evident: To the psalmist Yahweh means protection, refuge, salvation. Deuteronomy (32:15) called the Lord "Rock of Salvation," and David later did the same (Ps. 89:27).

Just like rock, other metaphors are used; one of these is "refuge," already met in Ps. 18:2, 3. We find this in the familiar verse of Ps. 46: "The Lord of hosts is with us; the God of Jacob is our refuge" (vv. 4, 8, 12).

People based their security on Yahweh; an old song interprets this in a more pastoral image less reminiscent of warfare — the shepherd (Ps. 23).

A shepherd is an idyllic figure for us; he is less so in the East. There the king is represented as the shepherd of the people and thus is transferred to Yahweh. Ps. 80 addresses him: "Give ear, O Shepherd of Israel, thou who leadest Joseph like a flock" (v. 2). He is shepherd because he acts for his flock, the people of Israel, and has its welfare in view (Ps. 74:1; 78:52; 79:13; 95:7; 100:3).

In Psalm 23 an individual voice sings the song of the shepherd: "The Lord is my shepherd, I shall not want; he makes me lie down in green pastures. He leads me beside still waters; he restores my soul. He leads me in paths of righteousness for his name's sake. Even though I walked through the valley of the shadow of death, I fear no evil; for thou art with me; thy rod and thy staff, they comfort me" (vv. 1-4).

This prayer certainly does not rise from a quiet, unruffled existence; it is not the language of one who can trust in God because there has never been anything blocking his path. It is the prayer of a person in real need. Enemies are threatening him, but with a leap he rises to God, to him who has repeatedly given the assurance: "I am with you" (cf. Gen. 24:3, 24; 28:15; 31:3; Deut. 31:6 ff.). As a shepherd defends his flock with his iron-studded club, and keeps it together with his staff, the Lord defends and leads his people.

The same author offers another concept in Ps. 23:5: "God is the host. He anoints the head of his guest, he fills the cups, gives him hospitality in his own house, that is, in his temple" (Ps. 15:1; 61:5).

God had spoken about his own love in the past, even compared it with the love of a mother who fondles and nourishes her little child: ". . . and I became to them as one who eases the yoke on their jaws, and I bent down to them and fed them" (Hos. 11:4).

A religious individual, one of the "Lord's poor" and averse to great plans, sings in the same key about his confident rest in the Lord: "Like a child quieted at its mother's breast; like a child that is quieted is my soul" (Ps. 131:2). Israel's prayer is

This plea is reminiscent of the ancient practice of taking refuge in the temple during persecution, making the house of the Lord an asylum, a refuge. It often is the only assurance of protection (cf. 1 Kings 2:28). This is the thought of the psalm, which begins with the trustful, "The Lord is my light and my salvation: whom shall I fear?" (Ps. 27). This pious petition expresses but one desire: to live in the house of the Lord and to taste his sweetness in silent contemplation. There is another advantage: in time of need one is certain of protection there; it is known that his tent is always a protecting cover: "For he will hide me in his shelter in the day of trouble; he will conceal me under the cover of his tent, he will set me high upon a rock" (verse 5).

We find this same sentiment in Psalm 61: "From the end of the earth I call to thee, when my heart is faint. Lead thou me to the rock that is higher than I; for thou art my refuge, a strong tower against the enemy. Let me dwell in thy tent for ever. O to be safe under the shelter of thy wings" (3:5).

"Set me high upon a rock": without a doubt this is a prayer for security. Rocks as shelters for fugitives play a protective role in the land of Canaan. Five kings of the Amorites sought safety in flight in the cave at Makkadah (Jos. 10, 16 ff.) and David found refuge in the caves of the desert of Judah. A rock was also inaccessible; it usually provided a favorite place for establishing almost impregnably strong cities. Such was Petra, the old rock-city in

nearby Edom: a whole town — houses, temples and
fortifications — was carved in the rock and formed
an unassailable fortress. Jerusalem of the Jebusites
was built on a projecting rock. The native inhabitants felt so safe there, that, when David besieged
the town, they cried to him: "You will not come in
here, but the blind and the lame will ward you off"
(2 Sam. 5:6). The temple of the Lord was built on
that rock.

Two psalms which deal with the protection within
the house of the Lord probably refer to the rock
on which the Ark of the Covenant, symbol of God's
presence, was definitively established.

It is not surprising that Yahweh himself, who
lived on that rock and to whom one took refuge
when pursued, was called "Rock" in a metaphorical
sense. Isaiah spoke about the "Rock of Israel" (30:29);
God is also referred to by the same name in the
ancient poem of 2 Sam. 23. He is the Rock in Deut.
32:4 and in verse 15: "When Jacob had eaten, and
was satisfied and Jeshiurun waxed fat, he kicked, and
he forsook God who made him, and scoffed at the
Rock of his salvation" (cf. vv. 18 and 37).

In the psalm literature the individual Israelite
often addresses his God as "my Rock": "I love thee,
O Lord, my strength. The Lord is my rock, and my
fortress, and my deliverer, my God, my rock, in
whom I take refuge, my shield, and the horn of my
salvation, my stronghold" (18:2, 3). In Psalm 31 the
fugitive prays: "Incline thy ear to me, rescue me

fice. Jeremiah clearly states: "They set up their abominations in the house which is called by my name, to defile it. They built the high places of Baal in the valley of the son of Hinnom, to offer up their sons and daughters to Moloch, though I did not command them, nor did it enter into my mind, that they should do this abomination to cause Judah to sin" (32:30-35).

The prophets hurled vehement accusations and reproaches against these practices. In the eighth century Hosea calls the attitude of Israel fornication. Jeremiah does the same. He speaks about the infidelity of the people; he contrasts it to the tender love of the time in the desert: "Oracle of the Lord! I remember the devotion of your youth, your love as a bride" (Jer. 2:2). He idealizes Israel's past and complains in the name of the Lord: "What wrong did your fathers find in me that they went far from me, and went after worthlessness, and became worthless?" (Jer. 2:5). He refers to the false prophets as fools profiteering in the name of Baal, stupid followers of powerless gods: "They have forsaken me, the fountain of living waters, and hewed out cisterns for themselves, broken cisterns, that can hold no water" (Jer. 2:13).

Israel sabotaged the most beautiful expectation of the Lord who wished to cherish them as children: ". . . a pleasant land, a heritage most beauteous of all nations. And I thought you would call me, My Father, and would not turn from following me, surely, as a faithless wife leaves her husband, so

have you been faithless to me, O house of Israel"
(Jer. 3:19-20).

Israel becomes his disloyal one, Judah the faithless. "Have you seen what she did, that faithless
one, Israel?" The Lord asks the prophets in the
days of King Josiah "how she went up on every
hill and under every green tree, and there played
the harlot? And I thought, after she has done all
this, she will return to me, but she did not return,
and her false sister Judah saw it. She saw that for
all the adulteries of the faithless one, Israel, I had
sent her away with a decree of divorce; (this indicates the fall of the Northern state in 722); yet her
false sister Judah did not fear, but she too went
and played the harlot. Because harlotry was so
light to her, she polluted the land committing
adultery with stone and tree. Yet for all this her
false sister Judah did not return to me with her
whole heart, but in pretense" (Jer. 3:6-10).

All reduces to the fact that the people have
turned their backs, rather than their faces, to the
Lord (Jer. 7:24; 32:33; cf. 2:27).

Ezekiel portrays Israel as the faithless bride.
Hosea and Jeremiah had already pointed with
definite melancholy to the years in the desert, when
Israel was satisfied with the Lord. Ezekiel does
not experience this. Egypt, the desert of the Sinai,
Canaan — no matter where Israel is, it is an adulterous generation (Ezek. 16:15-58; 20:1-44). The psalm-
ists also mention persons who see the clear light of

sensed the necessity of admonishing them to throw
away their idols. Many suppose that on this occasion
he admitted other tribes into the covenant who
opted for the Lord and accepted him as king. The
making of this pact consisted of a ceremony in which
Joshua guaranteed that the people would choose the
Lord. On Sinai Yahweh had taken the initiative to
adopt the people as his own; here in Sichem, Joshua
takes the initiative and urges the people to accept
the Lord again in their changed circumstances,
since they now are in the land of promise. He lays
down new laws, a further development of the
Mosaic law, over and above the charter of Moses
and erects a monument as a silent witness and a
permanent warning.

**Samuel:** When he is at the verge of handing over
the scepter of leadership to Saul, Samuel seriously
warns the people. Election of a king has, in his
opinion been tantamount to rejection of theocracy.
The people have shown their lack of confidence in
God. He has been indulgent, but Samuel hopes
that king and people will fear Yahweh and live
according to his commandments. If they do, they
will live. The people, impressed by his words and
by the sign he calls from heaven, are again con-
firmed in their love of the covenant (1 Sam. 12).

**David:** After David for the last time, assembles
the rulers of Israel along with the priests and
Levites he makes a farewell speech. He tells of
his plan to build a temple for the Lord, but that
Yahweh did not allow him to do so. His son Solomon

would build it. Yahweh himself has chosen Solomon
as his son and he will be a father to him. He will
confirm his mastery for ever, if he continues to
observe the Law as he has so far done. David
solemnly warns the leaders of Israel, in the presence
of the Lord, to keep the commandments. Then, and
only then, will they maintain possession of their
beautiful land and pass it on to their descendents
as a heritage (1 Chron. 28:2-8).

The last words and deeds of Israel's greatest
leaders are characterized by deep concern for the
destiny of their people.

## 4. Renewal of the covenant

Yahweh sometimes threatens; when the occasion
demands, he does more. Threats became a reality
when the people betray the covenant. General
disasters are his scourges, designed to ensure conversion of his people. According to the Deuteronomic
circles, the native inhabitants of Canaan who were
not conquered by Joshua are a test for the tribes
of Jacob, who had violated the covenant (cf. Judg.
2:20-23). The prophet Hosea also has the same conviction: God will permit more hardship for Israel,
his bride, in the hope that she will repent after
recognizing that the world has estranged her from
him. "Behold, I will allure her, and bring her into
the wilderness, and speak tenderly to her" (Hos. 2:16).

When the people feel the scourge of God, they
again follow their covenant with him. The history
of the southern state of Juda recounts episodes in

highest officials, scribes, seers, sooth-sayers and vassals of Assyria took the oath of loyalty.

Deuteronomy reminds us of the approaching death of Moses. He admonishes, enacts new laws, takes measures to keep the sons of Israel within the Law after crossing the Jordan and living among the heathens (Deut. 27:1-8). The people must set up large stones on Mount Ebal and whitewash them with lime, and write the words of the Law upon them. They must build an altar of stone to the Lord here. No iron tool is to be used; they shall offer burnt offerings. Then they shall sacrifice peace offerings, and shall eat and rejoice before the Lord. This same ceremony previously takes place within Canaan's boundaries (Jos. 8:30-35). To symbolize that Yahweh will rule the land of Canaan, his altar is erected in the heart of the highlands. His Laws are written on stone. But these symbols of the Lord are not enough; the Law must also live in the hearts of the people. Hence Moses decides that half of the tribes will ask for the blessing on Mount Gerizim, and that the other part will underline the curses with their "amen" on Mount Ebal.

It is possible that Deuteronomy is a literary fiction, utilized by seventh century reformers to give their movement a Mosaic foundation. But one fact is certain: Moses providentially tried to prepare for the future before his death in Moab.

**The spiritual testament of Joshua:** In his old age Joshua calls the elders, chiefs, judges and leaders

of Israel and speaks his last words which show concern for the salvation of his people. Moses had
endowed him with his spirit; we hear echoes of Moses
in Chapter 23 and following. He urges the leaders
to love God constantly because Israel's religion is
founded upon that love which is basic for their
welfare. If they cherish Yahweh, he will drive away
the hostile peoples resisting them in the heavily walled
towns of Canaan. But if they behave sinfully, these
enemies will become a scourge to them, a snare, a
thorn in their eye and will finally drive them from
the beautiful country.

His last act, motivated by his regard for the
future, is the making of the covenant by the assembly
of Sichem (chapter 24). This was to provide another
repetition of election by Yahweh. Therefore Joshua,
representative of the Lord, recalls what has been
done out of love for them. This is considerable.
He led Abraham from beyond the river, gave him
descendants, redeemed the children of Israel from
Egypt, gave them the land of Canaan in a series
of wonderful victories. The Lord then placed everything under their dominion even though they had
put no effort into the acquisition. He gave them
fields they did not plough, towns they did not build,
and vineyards and olive groves they did not plant.
After he enkindled their hearts with enthusiasm for
himself, he enjoined them to serve him faithfully
and sincerely and to abandon the gods they had
served in Egypt and on the other side of the river.

It is a curious thing nevertheless, that Joshua

God's mercy crossed by the dark shadow of Israel's infidelity (Ps. 78; 106; etc.).

**Externalism:** God expects more than a simple elementary fidelity from his bride. He wants her heart, for that is his commandment: "You shall love the Lord your God with all your heart, and with all your soul, and with all your might" (cf. Deut. 6:4). She must be interiorly committed to him. This was not the case with Israel. A merely exterior worship satisfied the people from the days of Isaiah to the time of Christ. The word of the eighth-century prophet: "This people draw near with their mouth, and honor me with their lips" (Is. 29:13) is also true in the days of Christ (cf. Mt. 15:8).

When the shadows of impending doom are lengthening over the people at the time of Jeremiah, they put their hope in the temple. They say: "The temple of the Lord, the temple of the Lord, the temple of the Lord is here" and they make no change in their way of living: injustice, oppression of strangers, orphans and widows, murder and other iniquities — all occur; they never bid farewell to their foreign gods. The prophet cries to them: "You trust in deceptive words" (Jer. 7:8). "Thus says the Lord of hosts, the God of Israel: Add your burnt offerings to your sacrifices, and eat the flesh. For in the day that I brought them out of the land of Egypt, I did not speak to your fathers or command them concerning burnt offerings and sacrifices. But this command I gave them: Obey my voice, and I will be your God, and you shall be my people; and walk in all the way that I command you, that it may be well with you" (Jer. 7:21-23).

Israel's vacillating faith is a source of concern for its leaders. Fulfillment of the promises rests on the faith and the favor of the Lord depends on it. At the making of the covenant Yahweh had promised his blessings: possession in futurity of a country flowing with milk and honey. He had also threatened: "Sudden terrors will come over them, consumption and fever, and the harvest, where for they worked hard, will be taken away by enemies; defeat after defeat. And if in spite of this they still will not hearken to me, the terrors will be sevenfold: drought, famine and the sword of the enemy" (cf. Lev. 26:14-39). Therefore Moses, Joshua, Samuel and other holy leaders strive to strengthen the people's faith, exhaust themselves in evoking their "Amen" to the Lord's covenant offer. Israel's very existence is in jeopardy.

### 3. Strengthening of the covenant faith

In their old age these leaders provided for continuation of the covenant. This reminds one of ancient Assyrian monuments describing how great rulers, builders of huge states, secured their dynasties as death approached. An old treaty document tells us that four years before he died Asarhddon, with fitting ceremony, appointed Assurbanipal as his successor. The royally attired crown-prince was led before the people and assigned the place reserved for the successor to the throne. Then the

which the leaders try to reestablish a proper relationship with the Lord and to ensure this they renew
the covenant oath.

King Ezechias, the successor to Achaz the weak-
ling, whose unbelief evoked catastrophe on Judah
and Jerusalem and opened it to ravishment by the
Assyrians, repairs the damage by making another
pact with the Lord: he orders the purification of the
sanctuary (2 Chron. 29:5-11) and, as champion of
the people, he once more binds himself to Yahweh.

King Josiah's covenant renewal in the last quarter
of the seventh century is well-known (2 Kings 22-23).
During his rule the Mosaic Law, almost completely
forgotten, was rediscovered. He reads about the
sanctions that follow contravention of the Laws
and is fearful because the people do not live according to its precepts. He, along with his people, makes
a covenant with the Lord, frightened as they are by
the threat of annihilation from Babylon.

We meet a final expression of covenant faith in
Jer. 34:8-22. Jerusalem is on the verge of being
besieged by Nabuchadnezzar. In this situation, king
Sedekiah decides to make a covenant with the Lord.
He and his people agree to comply with the Law.
ordering that Hebrew slaves be set free (cf. Jer. 34:13,
14). This is a beautiful gesture. But their changed
attitude after the tide turned is not so beautiful: they
revert to their previous skeptical stance. Iron chains
are their reward: the people are led captive into exile.

In this exile they experience what it means to abandon the Lord. During the Babylonian imprisonment they do not leave Yahweh for other gods, and yet their zeal for him is still far from perfect. They are habitually selfish and materialistic. This attitude, in the eyes of Esdras and Nehemiah, is the reason why they must continue to bend their backs for foreign rulers, and even after their return to the country Yahweh has destined for them they are slaves in their own homes. Therefore they make a written alliance: all — leaders, Levites and priests — agree to live according to the Law of the Lord. They take an oath that they will maintain the oft-repeated covenant; they will no longer give their daughters to the native inhabitants, or accept the daughters of Canaan as wives for their sons. They will not trade with the native people on the Sabbath and festival days. In the seventh year they will refrain from harvesting and prosecuting debtors. Finally, they will supply annual contributions for the maintenance of temple worship (Neh. 10:29-39; cf. Esd. 10).

Israel is repeatedly unfaithful, yet this adulterous bride keeps returning, time after time to her husband. This must be in accord with the plan of the Lord. He punishes her, he periodically abandons her to her own resources — but he never leaves her completely (Hos. 3:1-4), for he is a faithful God. Perennially, his word perdures and his plan to make Israel a holy people prevails.

# 4

## GOD KEEPS HIS WORD!

### 1. The fidelity of the Lord throughout history

The covenant is summarized in one pronouncement: "You shall be my people!" This includes a psychic alliance which in turn includes the reality that he will be with them; he makes himself responsible for them. He will make the people his **chesed;** he will abide by the agreement he has made. For Yahweh always says "amen" to his own word. The adjective **neeman** is typically expressive of the covenant's God (Deut. 7:9; 2 Sam. 7:28; Ps. 132:11, etc.). The verb from which it is derived means "stand firm"; for instance, it refers to pillars (2 Kings 18:16), and in a moral sphere it means to be faithful. The theme of the Lord's fidelity recurs so often that we could quote much of the Bible in this context. All salvation history takes place within the aegis of Yahweh's fidelity.

Speaking of the journey through the desert the Lord says: "I have led you for forty years through the desert. The clothes did not wear out on your body, neither the shoes on your feet. You did not need to eat bread nor to drink wine or spirits, that you should know that I am the Lord your God. And

when you came to this place, and Sichon, king of
Chesjbon, and Og, king of Basjan, fought against us,
we defeated them, occupied their country and we
gave the heritage to the sons of Ruben and Gad,
and to half of the family of Manasseh" (Deut. 27:4-8).

In reference to conquest of Canaan we read: "Thus
the Lord gave to Israel all the land which he swore
to give to their fathers; and having taken possession
of it, they settled there. And the Lord gave them
rest on every side just as he had sworn to their
fathers; not one of all their enemies had withstood
them, for the Lord had given all their enemies into
their hands. Not one of all the good promises which
the Lord had made to the house of Israel had failed;
all came to pass" (Jos. 21:43-45).

Psalm 105 is outstanding among the many psalms
in which the fidelity of the Lord is sung. In brilliant
style the poet portrays the history of Israel. From
Abraham to the period when it inherited the lands
of the heathens, Yahweh's word realizes itself: "To
you I will give the land of Canaan as heritage"
(verse 11).

In times of need the Lord raises up the judges,
men endowed with special qualities, to regain secure
possession of fields and vineyards for the people
(cf. 1 Sam. 12:11). They however do not have
enough confidence in their unpredictable champions,
they want a king.

Yahweh acquiesces and gives the people a king

to save them. Saul fails. His next choice is David:
"He took him from the sheepfolds; from tending the
ewes that had young he brought him to be the
shepherd of Jacob his people, of Israel his inheritance." Here the poet (Ps. 78-70-71) sees David's
kingship as a sign of the Lord's care for Israel, his
covenant partner. The new king acquires what
Yahweh had intended as the ideal country for
Israel. He found a realm reaching "from the wilderness and this Lebanon as far as the great river . . .
the Euphrates . . . toward the great sea" (Jos. 1:4 and
in Deut. 11:24).

David is an excellent instrument in God's hand,
because he is eminently faithful, unswerving in his
loyalty and steadfast in his service to the Lord.

**The covenant of David:** To realize Israel's destiny
as a holy people, a leaven for his kingdom on earth,
the Lord chooses the house of David. When this
man, in a quiet moment, shows his zeal for Yahweh
in expressing a desire to build a house for him, the
Lord does not leave this unrewarded: "I will make
for you a great name," is the oracle of the prophet
Nathan, "like the name of the great ones of the
earth; and I will appoint a place for my people
Israel, and will plant them, that they may dwell in
their own place, and be disturbed no more; and
violent men shall afflict them no more, as formerly
. . . When your days are fulfilled and you lie down
with your fathers, I will raise up your offspring
after you, who shall come forth from your body,
and I will establish his kingdom." Nathan says: "The

Lord shall build a house for you." The relationship will be such that God shall be a father to David, and his offspring will be the Lord's son. The result is that Yahweh will never reject the descendents of David; however, he will punish them if necessary (cf. 2 Sam. 7:8-16). The prophet does not use the word **berit,** yet this passage is recorded in history as a covenant. Later generations accept it as a true covenant — thus the author of David's "last words" (2 Sam. 23:5), the author of Chronicles (2 Chron. 13:5 and 21:7), the poet of Ps. 89 and Sirach (cf. 45:25). They have a reason for their acceptance. Yahweh's method in 2 Sam. 7 shows a willingness to enter into a covenant relationship with David. The opening lines (2 Sam. 7:8) mention his kindness in the past (7:8-9a) and contain his promises (7:9b-14a) and threats (verses 14b-15). There is also the statement: "I will be his father, and he shall be my son," reminiscent of the covenant formula, "I will be their God, and they will be my people."

Yahweh's pact with David includes a wider agreement — a solemn assurance that David's royal crown will be eternal, and that the kingdom which the Lord himself builds in Israel is to be perpetual.

**The conflict between faith and justice:** Hosea shows that many times the Lord begins anew with his unfaithful bride. On these occasions, God's faithfulness is always stronger than the infidelity of Israel. Yahweh reveals himself to Moses as, "a merciful and gracious God, slow to anger, and abounding in steadfast love and faithfulness, keeping steadfast love for thousands, forgiving iniquity and transgression and sin, but who will by no means clear the guilty, visiting the iniquity of the fathers upon the children and the children's children, to the third and the fourth generation" (Ex. 34:5-9).

Prophets speaking after Hosea, express this differently, in terms of a surviving "remnant." With Amos this thought is expressed as a hope (Amos 5:15); but for Isaiah and his contemporaries it is a positive conviction.

√ The pre-exilic prophets represent the remnant as the people who remain in the country after the Assyrian kings, Salmanassar, Sargon and Sennacherib capture the better element of the population. Isaiah says this in the story of his calling (6:1-13). The holy God sends him to awaken the people. Since this preaching eventually proves unsuccessful, his instructions read: "Make the hearts of this people fat, and their ears heavy, and shut their eyes . . ." Isaiah asks, "For how long?" and receives the answer, "Until cities be waste, without inhabitants, and houses without men, and the land is utterly desolate, and the Lord removes men far away and forsaken places are many in the midst of the land. And though a tenth remain in it, it will be burned again." This is strong language, but it is immediately softened by God's merciful fidelity: "Like a terebinth or an oak, whose stump remains standing when it is felled, the holy seed is its stump!" He is to give this concrete form by assigning his oldest son a symbolic name — "The rest will repent" (Is. 7:3). Other texts reflecting the remnant idea, are Is. 10:20-22; 11:11-16; 28:5; 4:2; Mich. 4:7; 5:6 ff.; Amos 9:8 ff.

The prophets of the exilic period consider the exiles themselves the remnant. These expect to return to the country of the promise where they will be the seed for a new generation. Jeremiah gives Yahweh's proclamation: "At the time, says the Lord, I will be the God of all the families of Israel, and they shall be my people . . . The people who survived the sword found grace in the wilderness (this is, on their return from Babel (when Israel sought for rest" (Jer. 31:1-2; cf. Jer. 3:14; Ezek. 14:22; Soph. 3:13; Joel 3:5).

After the exile, remnant refers to the repatriates (Esd. 9:8; 13-15; Zech. 8:11; 13:8 ff.) or in the texts concerning the day of the Lord, those who are left on the last day (Zech. 14:2). The Lord will never be so angry that none of his chosen ones will remain. He will realize his salvation plans in this Remnant.

## 2. Prophetic visions of the future

The covenant idea of Israel as Yahweh's own possession, taken into his sphere, contained the promise that the people would be the unmolested owners of a land so fruitful that they could live in royal splendor. There is disappointment; they do indeed experience good times, but quite frequently they differ. The prophets see Yahweh's punishment for unfaithfulness in this. They see a return and attach great future expectation to it. Israel is a nation orientated to the future as well as to the past.

Its expectation is based on belief in the living God from whom it previously had always obtained salvation. This realistic concept of a faithful Lord developed in the prophets an inner certainty that some day he would give covenant peace for ever.

There shall be peace! They do not have a clear idea of the type of peace that will come nor how it will occur. They picture events to the imagination of the people in language typical of their time. These can be judged as too idealistic for present-day tastes, but the essence of their message is important: There shall be peace.

They picture the future as a time when man will never again be disturbed by animals, drought, or an enemy's sword. Nature will be subject to the people. "On that day," the Lord says, "I will make for you a covenant with the beasts of the field, the birds of the air, and the creeping things of the ground" (Hos. 2:20a); a covenant, where creatures will no longer disturb man.

The land of Jezreel, cursed because the downfall of the northern state began there, and the dynasty of Jehu who succeeded to the throne, prompted the people to apostasize from the Lord; but this land will again produce grain, wine and oil (cf. Hos. 2:23-24).

The imagery of the prophet Isaiah in this regard is striking and familiar: "The wolf shall dwell with the lamb, and the leopard shall lie down with the kid, and the calf and the lion and the fatling together, and a little child shall lead them. The cow and the bear shall feed; their young shall lie down together; and the lion shall eat straw like the ox. The suckling child shall play over the hole of the asp, and the weaned child shall put his hand on the adder's den" (Is. 11:6-8).

Ezekiel uses the same description about the year 600: "I will make with them a covenant of peace and banish wild beasts from the land, so that they may dwell securely in the wilderness and sleep in the woods. And I will send down the showers in their season; they shall be showers of blessing. And the trees of the field shall yield their fruit, and the earth shall yield its increase" (Ezek. 34:25-27).

Inimical neighbors will be curbed. "I will abolish the bow, the sword and war from the land; and I will make you lie down in safety" (Hos. 2:20b).

The prophet Isaiah is emphatic on this point, because in his time the battle-hardened Assyrians with their awesome cavalry were terrorizing the East. He proclaims light in the darkness for the area around the lake of Galilee. The Lord will lift the burden from their shoulders and break the rod of their oppressor (Is. 9:1-4). The child, called Immanuel, will be the instrument of this. We can rejoice, the prophet says, "For to us a child is born, to us a son is given, and the government will be upon his shoulder, and his name will be called: Wonderful Counselor, Mighty God, Everlasting Father, Prince of Peace. He will bring great power and enduring

peace to the throne of David, and over his kingdom"
(Is. 9:5, 6; cf. 11:1-5).

A century later, when the Babylonians tore up the
land as with a ploughshare and transported the
most important citizens of Israel to the banks of
Babylon's streams, the spirit of the Lord came over
Jeremiah and Ezekiel. Like Isaiah, both proclaim a
new David who shall be instrumental in destroying
the enemy.

Jeremiah says: "It shall come to pass on that day,
that I will break the yoke from off their neck, and
I will burst their bonds, and strangers shall no more
make servants of them. But they shall serve the
Lord their God and David their king, whom I will
raise up from them" (30:8, 9; cf. Ezek. 34:23-24 and
37:24). There will be no more threats. Nothing will
be able to harm Israel in the future.

Isaiah associates this with the merciful care of the
Lord. As Yahweh safeguarded the people in the
exodus with a cloud by day and a fiery pillar by
night, so all Zion and its surroundings will be pro-
tected in the future. "Then the Lord will create over
the whole side of Mount Zion and over her assem-
blies a cloud by day, and smoke and the shining of
a flaming fire by night" (Is. 4:5). However, this
will be founded upon the restoration of good relations with the Lord, for, the prophet says, it will
happen "when the Lord shall have washed away the
filth of the daughters of Zion and cleansed the
bloodstains of Jerusalem" (Is. 4:4).

Thus the prophets speak about the restoration of the covenant. Hosea says that the Lord will engage himself with the people for ever, in justice and law, in mercy and in faith, and it will know the Lord. This is not only an intellectual knowledge but a commitment owed to God, a loving knowledge.

Jeremiah accepts this. However, he carries the thought considerably further: God will make another completely new pact with the people. This is original with Jeremiah; he explains how it will be realized. The old situation will be destroyed. The Old Covenant has become a farce; the exile of the people is the best proof of this: the people were not holy; the Law was consistently broken. It was no longer identified with their very flesh and blood but degenerated into externals. As a result, it was an incitement to opposition. Jeremiah knew the bitter experience of Paul: I do what I do not want to do: the heart is a furnace of rebellion against God's will. In the new era it will be different: disharmony between God's will and human inclinations will vanish; the people will serve God's cause as their own; they will experience the Law as being within themselves. "Behold, the days are coming," is the oracle of God, "when I will make a new covenant with the house of Israel and the house of Judah; a new covenant, not like the covenant which I made with their fathers when I took them by the hand to bring them out of the land of Egypt, my covenant which they broke. But this is the covenant which I will make with the house of Israel after those days, says the Lord: I will put my law within them, and I will write it upon their hearts; and I will be their God, and they shall be my people" (Jer. 31:31-33). In the future God will regard his people individually; each one will know him: "And no longer shall each man teach his neighbor and each his brother, saying, Know the Lord, for they shall all know me, from the least of them to the greatest" (31:34).

A few years later Ezekiel says almost the same in his own words. God will establish an everlasting covenant (cf. Ezek. 16:60). He places this immediately after the exile. When the Lord has gathered them from all the nations, "he will sprinkle clean water upon them; and he will clean them from all their uncleannesses . . . A new heart I will give you and a new spirit I will put within you; and I will take out of your flesh the heart of stone. And give you a heart of flesh. And I will put my spirits within you, and cause you to walk in my statutes and be careful to observe my ordinances. You shall dwell in the land which I gave to your fathers; and you shall be my people, and I will be your God" (Ezek. 36:25-28). The covenant will have a new foundation, the gift of the Spirit who will inspire the people to do holy deeds and will enable them to maintain the laws. As they already knew, the Spirit of the Lord enabled the people to do superhuman deeds. With this Spirit they will again share in the power and holiness of Yahweh (cf. Is. 11:2-3; Ps. 51:13).

When the covenant is kept, there is holiness.

Isaiah speaks about this virtue in connection with
Mount Zion at the time when the "sprout" of the
Lord, the shoot from Jesse's stem will appear. All
who are recorded in the civil register of Jerusalem
will be holy (Is. 4:2-3). Holiness is the work of the
"sprout," who is the new David: As a fruit of his
government "they shall not hurt or destroy in all
my holy mountain; for the earth shall be full of the
knowledge of the Lord, as the waters cover the sea"
(Is. 11:9).

During the exile another prophet appears. His
real name is unknown but he writes like Isaiah,
and he adds to his predecessor's book the oracles
that came to him in the last period of the exile.
He is called Deutero-Isaiah or Second Isaiah. Some
texts are scattered throughout Is. 1-39, but most are
concentrated in chapters 40 to 55. He speaks about
future salvation as a repetition of the delivery from
Egypt (cf. Is. 33:22; 35:4). He tells about the re-
construction of Zion and about heathen participation
in the worship of the Lord. But we are especially
interested in the songs of the Servant of Yahweh.
These four songs are in 42:1-6; 49:1-9; 50:4-9; 52:13–
53:12).

He describes the Servant as a prophet, filled with
the Spirit of God, proclaiming the law of the Lord,
to Israel as well as to distant peoples. God led him
by the hand, led him into his service and gave him
as a covenant to the people and a light to the nations
(Is. 42:1-6). He is the covenant mediator who will
bring salvation and lead Israel back to Zion. This

will also include interior conversion to the Lord. He will lead the blind and mentally unenlightened heathens to the light of God (49:8, 9). The fourth song, the most important, pictures him as a humble servant, who grows like a shapeless little twig, like a root from the thirsty ground, without form or splendor, ungracious, a man of sorrow. He is the servant who gives his life as a sin-offering for many (53:10). But he will be glorified by the Lord, and he whose appearance was marred beyond human recognition becomes a king before whom other potentates shall be silent (cf. 52:15). Like a king he shall see his offspring, he shall prolong his days, free from griefs and filled with knowledge (cf. 53:10b, 11a). In these songs the poet refers to a person who ,suffers for the sins of the people. The model of this future servant is probably Moses, who was also willing to take upon himself the guilt of his people (cf. Ex. 32:9 ff.).

The description of the servant as the covenant mediator is the culminating point of Old Testament expectation. In later years this hope for a new everlasting pact is repeated, as for example, in Is. 61:1; 62:12. This reaches a climax in the words of Mal. 3:1, "The Lord whom you seek will suddenly come to his temple; the messenger of the covenant in whom you delight, behold, he is coming, says the Lord of hosts."

Ancient Christian authors see these expectations fulfilled in Jesus, the Child of the Virgin from Nazareth.

# 5

# THE NEW COVENANT

"Wretched man that I am!, who will deliver me from this body of death?" (Rom. 7:24).

This cry of distress comes from one who to his dismay finds that he is imprisoned by the power of evil, and is a slave of sin. To grasp exactly what Paul means by the "body of death," we must understand the semitic mentality which never sees anything in isolation, but always in some sort of unity and association. The sin which now tyrannizes man is the sin of Adam. In itself it is a transgression, like any other sin, but because it is the transgression of a father, it is passed on to the community inseparably linked with him through ties of blood. Like a drop of ink on blotting-paper it spreads and infects all descended from Adam. This is the law of solidarity, strongly felt by all semitic peoples (cf. the case of Achan in Jos. 7:16-26).

Sin is an oppressing power because of its effects: interior disharmony, guilt, unleashed passions; we see the first examples in the murder of Cain, the vengefulness and unbridled lust of Lamech (Gen. 4).

When a semite says "sin" he thinks of the penalty which is inseparable from it. Adam's sin was punished by expulsion from paradise, suffering and death, laboring in the sweat of his brow. Expulsion from paradise means separation from communion with God. The garden in which Adam and Eve were placed is not an ordinary one but the most extraordinary on earth. In it is the tree of life. Whoever eats of it will always stay alive (cf. Gen. 3:22). There are no trees like this in our orchards. As a favor man is allowed to eat from it, but it really produces fruit for beings possessing a different way of life — heavenly beings. In the middle of the garden is the tree of the knowledge of good and evil. That gives omniscience. "The knowledge of good and evil" is a Hebraic expression for "knowledge of everything." People are not allowed the fruit of this tree. It is intended for heavenly beings. But this tree stands in paradise. This gives the impression that the garden of Eden is a heavenly one and this is accentuated by the fact that at certain times God walks there (Gen. 3:8) and also that, after the expulsion of the people, cherubim watch over the entrance with flaming swords. These cherubim, heavenly beings, obviously belong there. All this leads us to conclude that paradise was more a heavenly than an earthly garden. The graden of Eden is properly called the Garden of God (Is. 51:3 and Ezek. 28:13). Thus the favor of the Lord was that he transplanted man from the earthly fields in which he belonged into his own garden. The idea is obvious: the author wants to say that God adopted man. We could express the same concept by saying that God took man into his own home.

The sin of Adam with all its results becomes a vital force which infects every person from his youth (cf. Gen. 8:21) or, as Ps. 51 says, from the moment of birth, and it weighs upon all.

Paul asks, "Who will save me?" With a relieved mind he answers: "Thanks be to God, through Jesus Christ our Lord!" (Rom. 7:25). "There is therefore now no condemnation for those who are in Jesus Christ. For the law of the spirit of life in Christ Jesus has set you free from the law of sin and death" (Rom. 8:1, 2).

## 1. The Spirit

The Spirit of God who hovered over the waters and drew life from them (Gen. 1:2), the Spirit who breathed over the valley of bones and gave them back flesh and life (Ezek. 37:1-14), who was to elevate the offspring of the house of David to the status of a mighty king, omniscient judge and supreme priest (the contents of Is. 11:1-3), the Spirit who sanctifies (Ps. 51:12-14), who was promised by Ezekiel as a gift of the messianic time — this Spirit gives strength to conquer the power of evil.

The Spirit characterizes the New Covenant: Paul calls himself its minister; it is realized "not in a written code but in the Spirit" (2 Cor. 3:6; Rom. 7:6; Gal. 3:3; 4:29).

God's love is shown in the gift of the Spirit (Rom. 5:5), for in him we are able to address him as "Abba, Father" (Rom. 8:15; Gal. 4:6); when he sustains us, we can pray, because he himself intercedes for us

with a plea too deep for words (Rom. 8:26). He
causes his own effects in us: love, joy, peace, patience,
kindness, goodness, faithfulness, gentleness and self-
control (cf. Gal. 5:22).

The covenant is no longer uncertain. Its promise
of life has been assured. There it is called "the
better covenant" by the author of the letter to the
Hebrews (Heb. 8:6; cf. 7:22).

The gift of the Spirit is also the guarantee for
the realization of the covenant promises. He is the
pledge of future glory. In Rom. 8:23 Paul says that
we have received his first fruits. We should recall
what the Jews mean by the first fruits: they represent all which will follow. When they are dedicated
to the Lord everything else is included. Christians
still sigh in the body and they must suffer; they do
not prosper on this earth and wonder when salvation
will come. Paul shows them that they have already
received the first fruits of the life-giving Spirit and
this allows them to hope for the fullness of salvation (cf. 2 Chron. 1:22; 5:5; Eph. 1:14). The Spirit
is the beginning of our resurrection: "If the Spirit
of him who raised Jesus from the dead dwells in
you, he who raised Christ Jesus from the dead will
give life to your mortal bodies also through his
Spirit which dwells in you" (Rom. 8:11; cf. 1 Cor.
15:44).

**The Spirit, a gift from Christ:** The Spirit is a gift
from the exalted Lord who, when he was taken up
into heaven, sent the Spirit received from the Father.

This took place on the first Pentecost, when he came down upon the witnesses of all his works (Acts 2:33). He startled the world by making fishermen masters of the full word and meaning of scripture.

John tells that Christ stands in the middle of the temple on the Feast of Tabernacles and informs the feasting Jews that he is the Source of living water. "If any one thirst, let him come to me and drink. He who believes in me, as the scripture has said: Out of his heart shall flow rivers of living water." The evangelist explains that he is alluding to the Spirit which those who believed in him would receive. "Would" — because the Spirit was not yet there because Jesus was not yet glorified (Jn. 7:37-39).

"In Christ Jesus" one has the Spirit and his power is the way of escape from the oppressive domination of sin. This is what Paul says in Rom. 8:2, but he then continues: ". . . what the law, weakened by the flesh, could not do (we know that the prophets Jeremiah and Ezekiel had already noted this, and, instructed by the Spirit, had offered a solution) God has done, sending his own Son in the likeness of sinful flesh and for sin, he condemned sin in the flesh . . ." (8:3). He alludes here to Christ's crucifixion. At first sight we do not see any connection between these two sentences. What does the death of Christ have to do with it? Did death bring forth the principle of the new creation? Death is destructive, not creative. This is certain.

The question is resolved by meditation on the nature of life after the resurrection. This is not completely new, as it was at the dawn of creation; it is renewed. We might say that the old life is buried and may refer here to the body of Christ. It was necessary to tear down this body first, before it could be rebuilt. "Destroy this temple, and in three days I will raise it up" (Jn. 2:19). The new rises on the ruins of the old. Christ must first give his life, in keeping with a law he himself affirmed: "Unless a grain of wheat falls into the earth and dies, it remains alone; but if it dies, it bears much fruit" (Jn. 12:24). We can give another version of this: if people do not love, if married people are unwilling to make a self-offering, no new generation will arise; but those who have given themselves will become the source of life for others.

In this way Christ gave himself up so as to be able to give life to others.

In the Old Testament the poet of the Servant of Yahweh foresaw the fate of Christ. He described the Servant as a man listening to God early in the morning, who hears every word, absorbs it and passes it on to the people; welcome or unwelcome, he will not compromise with the truth and with God's will. The Servant is rejected, pursued and killed. This is the common lot of a prophet (cf. Mt. 23:29-35). His is a death for the iniquities of many. But then, too late, he is recognized and nations respect him.

Ancient Christian authors discovered Christ in

this description. When Jesus cured a crowd of sick
one evening, Matthew saw this as the fulfillment of
a verse from the fourth Servant-song, that "He took
our infirmities and bore our diseases" (8:17). He
delineates in Christ the character of the Servant:
not a rumor-monger, not a quarreler, not one who
breaks the bruised reed, or quenches a smoldering
wick (21:17-21). This assertion is based on the
witness God bore to him at the river Jordan and on
the Mount of glorification: "This is my beloved Son
with whom I am well pleased" (Mt. 3:17; 17:5) and
on the words spoken by Christ himself, borrowing
from Is. 53:10, 13: "The Son of Man came not to be
served, but to serve, and to give his life as a ransom
for many" (Mt. 20:28).

## 2. The blood of the New Covenant

At the Last Supper Jesus prays over the cup:
"Drink of it, all of you; for this is my blood of the
covenant, which is poured out for many for the forgiveness of sins" (Mt. 26:28). He alludes to the fourth
song of the Servant of Yahweh, (by his use of the
phrase "for many"), and to the tradition of Ex. 24:3-8
at least in Matthew's narrative of the event. Moses
presents the solemn covenant oath as preceded by
offerings to propitiate the Lord. Bulls and goats take
the place of the people. When Moses sprinkles the
Israelites with the blood, this takes them up into
the sphere of the Lord and wrests them from the
powerful sphere of evil because they are consecrated
by the blood of the sacrificial animals.

The blood of Christ is also sprinkled on the

people. But it has an infinitely greater vital efficacy.
The theologian who wrote the letter to the Hebrews
says, "For if the sprinkling of defiled persons with
the blood of goats and bulls . . . sanctifies for the
purification of the flesh, how much more shall the
blood of Christ, who through the eternal Spirit
offered himself without blemish to God, purify your
conscience from dead works to serve the living
God!" (Heb. 9:13-14). He says that Christ, the mediator of a New Covenant, brought release for the
transgressions committed under the first Covenant.
Paul formulates this precisely in Rom. 3:25: "He
was put forward by God as an expiation by his
blood." This emphasizes God's righteousness; with
divine forbearance he overlooks former sins to show
that now he himself is the righteous one and that
he justifies all who have faith in him. Paul first
notes that one might have the impression that God
is not holy (righteous) because in the past he let the
sinners in peace. But then he retorts that he could
do this, because he intended eventually to send his
Son who would wipe out sins.

Christ's offering has the character of atonement.
Those who unite themselves with him and are
sprinkled with his sacrificial blood will really be
cleansed internally.

The efficacy of the blood of Christ is described
in many ways.

We have already heard that the Spirit made
man free. Sin, as Paul presents it, has kept him

imprisoned, in slavery (Rom. 6:7, 16, 19, 20). But now, through the blood of Christ, all are redeemed (1 Cor. 6:20; 7:23). Nothing was initially required of man himself; the redemption was freely given (Rom. 3:24; Eph. 1:7; Col. 1:14). Peter says the same: "You know that you were ransomed from the futile ways inherited from your fathers, not with perishable things such as silver or gold, but with the precious blood of Christ . . ." (1 Pet. 1:18, 19). Christ had already spoken of a ransom for many (Mt. 20:28; Mk. 10:45). This repeats the Old Testament story of the liberation from Egypt. Through this Israel became God's own possession. The same is true of us — cf. 1 Cor. 6:19, "You are not your own."

Through the blood we have peace with God. Christ's death means atonement. This concept found only in Paul, gives us the knowledge that sin is a condition of animosity between God and us. We should actually mention ourselves first, because we, the people, were the source of this condition. On the contrary, atonement originates with the Lord. "While we were enemies we were reconciled to God by the death of his Son" (Rom. 5:10). From enemies we became friends. In 2 Cor. 5:18 the atonement is given as the reason why we are new creatures.

Christ reconciled two parties, which is the same as saying that he made peace. Two texts show the parallel between atonement and making peace. Col. 1:20 and Eph. 2:15.

Colossians has an idea, strange to us, that God

reconciled to himself not only humanity but the
entire universe, including the heavenly. Christ made
this peace through the blood of the cross (1:20). But
did the heavenly beings sin? Or can we say that
celestial beings, influenced by evil, were stirred up
by the sins of the people? It is an accepted fact
that the ground was cursed because of humanity,
and that man is spoken of as dust (Gen. 3:17-19).
The prophets describe a salvation in which the ma-
terial world participates (cf. Is. 11:7-9). But is there
a similar relationship between human beings and
angels? In later Jewish writings we see indications
of this: In Dan. 10-13 the angel of Israel, a heavenly
representative and protector of the country, must
do battle against the angel of Persia. The author
of Revelation directs the words of the Lord to the
angel of the Church in Ephesus, in Smyrna, etc.
These might be personifications of the guardian
angels of these communities. They share in the
glory or the degradation of the communities they
represent. We may have to pursue this line of
thought to explain atonement between God and
angels.

In Eph. 2:15 Jesus' salvific act includes Jews and
heathens. Paul tells the Ephesians, formerly heathens,
about the richness of their vocation, how they were
far from God in the past, without claim on Christ,
without a covenant and its promise of salvation; they
were outside of Israel, without promise, without
hope, without God. Now, however, they are close to
him. Christ "our peace" effected this. "He who has

made us both one, and has broken down the dividing wall of hostility, by abolishing in his flesh the Law of commandments and ordinances, that he might create in himself one new man in place of the two, so making peace, and might reconcile us both to God in one body through the cross, thereby bringing the hostility to an end. And he came and preached peace to you who were far off and peace to those who were near" (2:14-17). We were excluded from communion with the Father because of sin; in the Spirit we now have access to the same Father. Christ Jesus opened the door; we may come home again.

Paul says (Rom. 5:9) that through the Spirit we are guaranteed personal resurrection. This is resurrection to life. We need not be fearful of threatening wrath because we were freed when we came to Christ.

The crucifixion is the beginning of the New Covenant; Christ's death broke the power of evil; his offering replaces all Old Covenant sacrifices, making them mere foreshadowings. That is why this sacrifice on the cross exceeds that which Moses offered on Sinai as preparation for the covenant; it also represents the daily offerings of the worshiping people and the slaughtered paschal lamb, whose blood saved Israel from death.

Christian tradition regards Christ as the Paschal Lamb of the new time. Paul writes to the church of the Corinthians: "Christ, our paschal lamb, has been sacrificed" (5:7). In the fact that Christ died while the paschal lambs were being slaughtered in the temple, John sees Christ becoming the true Paschal Lamb from then on.

## 3. How we share in this New Covenant

Paul gives a two-fold answer to the question of how we can share in the release, the atonement, the peace of mind, acquired by Christ through his crucifixion: through faith and baptism. At one time he emphasizes faith, at another baptism. When he treats faith separately especially in Romans and Galatians — there is a controversial tendency.

Other New Testament authors, not as argumentative as he is, speak simply about faith and baptism. Mark says "He who believeth and is baptized, shall be saved" (16:16). We remember the words of John: "But to all who received him, who believed in his name, he gave power to become children of God" (1:12); we remember too his word to Nicodemus: "Truly, truly, I say to you, unless one is born anew, he cannot see the kingdom of God" (3:5).

**Faith according to Paul:** the legal attitude and pride of the Jews irritated Paul. They were obsessed with the Law (torah). When speaking of the covenant, they thought in terms of the Law and steadfastly maintained a conviction that it somehow gave them a claim on God's help. They expected salvation through faith in the Law. This resulted in a personal-achievement fixation and self-conceit. Paul opposes true faith to the pharisaic attitude. In his book **Biblical Spirituality** W. Grossouw has a detailed description of the apostle's concept of faith. It is the people's answer to the mercy of God in Christ, who is proclaimed in the gospels and in the preaching of the Apostles. The simplest formula is "a Christian believes the Gospel." Hence it follows immediately that this faith is not at all irrational but has an intellectual content. Its object is Christ who died for our sins and arose from death on the third day (1 Cor. 15:3-11). God justifies the ungodly (Rom. 4:5); Jesus is the Lord (Rom. 10:9). "For Paul, belief includes recognition of one's own incapability and sinfulness and the recognition of God's power, mercy and grace."[12] One who believes necessarily knows that God can give salvation; he will trust only in God. Paul views faith as the basis of a personal relationship with God. Knowing that God is infinitely good gives one reason to believe that he also will be well received. In the same way belief that God saves people leads to belief that he also will save an individual. "I believe you" must be equivalent to "I have faith in you, I trust you, I depend on you, I accept you completely."[13] This kind of faith contains love; it is surrender. Christ lives in my heart through faith (cf. Eph. 3:17).

In his letter to the Galatians Paul opposes justification through faith to the effect achieved through works of the Law. He establishes the absolute superiority of the New Covenant over the Old. Gal. 4:21-31 shows that the Law itself teaches this. The argumentation in this text is too often insufficiently understood. Although it probably was extremely meaningful for the rabbis it is too obscure for most of us. Paul begins with the Biblical statement that Abraham had two sons, one from a slave and one from a free-born woman. The slave Hagar, the mother of Ismael and of the Arabian peoples, symbolized by Mount Sinai which is situated in Arabia, is a prefiguration of the Jews who cling to the Law of Sinai. The free-born Sarah, a sterile woman who gave birth to the child Isaac through God's power, is a symbol of the new Jerusalem — the Church, created by the Lord. In this symbolic interpretation Paul is influenced by a text from Isaiah: "Sing, O barren one, who did not bear; break forth into singing and cry aloud, you who have not been in travail!" (54:1). Hagar and her child are opposed to Sarah and her offspring. The Bible gives the heritage to Isaac. It says, "Send away the slave and her son, for the son of the slave shall not inherit together with the son of the free-born." Paul concludes that those who have faith are the sons of the free woman and heirs of the salvation promise. They are not servants of the Law.

**Baptism.** On Pentecost, after Peter gave his first sermon and deeply moved his listeners, the question is asked, "Brethren, what shall we do?" Peter answered, "Repent, and be baptized every one of you in the name of Jesus Christ for the forgiveness of your sins" (Acts 2:38). If one wishes to share in the sacrifice of Christ, he must be baptized.

In Rom. 6:1-11 Paul explains the symbolism of baptism, making it the foundation for his argumentation: we may no longer give way to sinful egoism, but from now on must live for God. Baptism is a symbol of Christ's burial and resurrection. Paul says to the Christians: "Do you know that all of us who have been baptized into Christ Jesus were baptized into his death? We were buried therefore with him by baptism into death, so that as Christ was raised from the dead by the glory of the Father, we too might walk in newness of life" (6:3-4). "Baptized" means, above all, having died, being dead, removed. In the semitic world water images great terror, threatening power (cf. Ps. 69:2, 3: "Save me, O God!, for the waters have come up to my neck . . ."). Christ points to his suffering in baptismal images. He asks the jealous sons of Zebedee, "Are you able to drink the cup that I drink, or to be baptized with the baptism with which I am baptized?" (Mk. 10:38) and in the face of approaching death he says, "I have a baptism to be baptized with; and how I am constrained until it is accomplished" (Lk. 12:50).

Originally, baptism was by immersion. This signified that one put aside his old nature. His coming from the water manifested his will to begin life as a renewed creature, as a newly created being.

Romano Guardini says: "Water is a picture of death and life; or more exactly: of the grave in which the old life dies and the womb from which the new life rises."[14] Baptism administered by the Church in the name of Christ is not only an external symbol,

but also a real mystery. It is Christ who immerses
and lifts up the believer. It is he who gives real
power to this immersion and recovery. "He who
surrenders in faith," Guardini says, "will be born to
a new existence. The human being, who already
exists, is drawn into the deep womb of mercy and
rises again, sharing in a life proceeding from God."[15]

Baptism therefore is the sacrament of rebirth,
Paul writes to Titus (3:5) and Christ explains to
Nicodemus (Jn. 3:5). Reborn through divine power,
one enters into communion with God in a way never
considered possible in the Old Testament.

## 4. The new people of God

On Sinai the entire people of Israel became the
people of God; it was the choice of its masses. The
whole people promised to uphold the Law of God.

The new salvation demands a personal choice
because faith is a question of personal commitment.
One is grafted into Christ through faith. The sancti-
fying water causes the believer to participate in the
Spirit. From Christ he receives the "life-giving-
Spirit" (cf. 1 Cor. 15:45).

A little twig from an old tree is grafted on a new
one and lives from its sap of life; in the same way
we live from the trunk which is Christ, although
we do not completely lose our old independence.
John expresses this literally "I am the vine, you are
the branches" (15:5).

Paul uses the example of the body to indicate the

unity of life with Christ. "So we, though many, are one body in Christ, and individually members one of another" (Rom. 12:5; cf. 1 Cor. 12:12, 27).

We doubt that this view of identification with Christ was universal at the outset of Christianity. But it is certain that the Pentecost community was aware that it was a new people of God, the holy people, of whom the prophets had spoken.

They were assured of being heirs of the covenant promise God made with Abraham: they were the first-born of God, to whom he sent his servant as a blessing (Acts 3:25, 26). Christians had heard from the Jews that it is not natural descent what makes them the heirs of the promises; it is faith. Through faith they belong to Israel and are the offspring of Abraham. Those who persist in unbelief will be cut off from the trunk (Rom. 9:4). They will be disinherited because they frustrate their own salvation. Paul however thinks that after the heathens have welcomed salvation, the Jews will abandon their impenitence, for he believes that God will keep his word as spoken by Isaiah, namely, that the Savior will come forth out of Zion and that he will banish the godlessness from Jacob (Rom. 11:25, 26).

Through faith Israel is the ideal state, the covenant people. Other nations share in their benefits and thus through faith they also will belong to Israel.

All churches are conscious that they are a continuation of the Old Testament worship community.

In the Old Testament they spoke about the **qahal Jahweh,** in the Greek translation **ekklesia Kyriou.** This is Israel in its totality. Sometimes a given assembly comes to mind, other times the assembly around the revelation tent, the cult-communion (Deut. 23:2-4; 23:9; Neh. 13:1 etc.). All Christian communities are now addressed as **ekklesia.**

The first Christians are called "saints," because they are members of the holy people dedicated to God (1 Cor. 6:1; Rom. 8:26; 16:2 etc.); they are also called "elected and beloved" (Mt. 24:31; Rom. 8:33; Col. 3:12 etc.).

In connection with the covenant terminology of Ex. 19:6, Peter summarizes much when he says to the Christians: "But you are a chosen race, a royal priesthood, a holy nation, God's own people . . ." (1 Pet. 2:9).

The Church of Christ is the covenant people of the new salvation period, the people in whom God establishes his kingdom.

## 5. The Covenant and the Sermon on the Mount

A people filled with the Spirit should live according to the Spirit. This is Paul's conviction (Rom. 6:1-8, 17). In trying to picture for ourselves life according to the Spirit we might give our imagination free reign and will probably arrive at something similar to the vision of Jeremiah or Ezekiel, that a person lives from the inside out — that he who has made a home for God's Law in his heart will also maintain it.

Our thoughts would then constantly have God as their object. We would rise with him and go to sleep with him. Our will would correspond with his will at all times, as with a friend who does what the other asks purely out of love. We would love God as we love a person. We would rejoice in experiencing his nearness, and if this could not be, we would be homesick for him. We would belong to him heart and soul, not as a slave belonged to his master in times past — slavery is contrary to his will — but as a bride belongs to her husband. We would stand in the service of the Lord.

We could also reflect on life in the Spirit by considering its fruits, as Paul did. It is a living in love, joy, peace, patience, kindness, goodness, faithfulness, gentleness and self-control; one would then have crucified his selfishness and evil desires (cf. Gal. 5:22-24).

But we can also revert to the Sermon on the Mount in Matthew. The covenant mediator of the new salvation period proclaimed his conditions on the mountain, as Moses did. Christ corrects and perfects the old Law. He sees the holiness ideals of the Old Testament as in the bud, but now demands their fullness, "You have heard that it was said to the men of old, you shall not kill, and whoever kills shall be liable to judgment. But I say to you that every one who is angry with his brother shall be liable to judgment; whoever insults his brother shall be liable to the council, and whoever says, You fool, shall be liable to the hell of fire" (Mt. 5:21, 22).

This is a radical prohibition, not easy to measure up to. For a person who lives in this world it will be difficult but he can always reach for it.

The Master is just as radical in his other demands. He aims high, making the very perfection of the Father the norm of our conduct (Mt. 5:48).

Practical devotion may not be 'merely external; it must come from the heart. One's intention must be pure: when he prays, he must lock himself up in his room; when he fasts, he should use make-up, put on a "fresh face"; and when he gives alms, his left hand should not know what his right hand is doing (Mt. 6:1-18).

Christ speaks about the feelings and deeds which characterize this new life — detachment from earthly things, freedom for God, confidence in his providence, a reliance on him which is foolish, according to earthly standards (Mt. 6:19; 7:23).

The word of Christ came to a world estranged from God, and controlled by the devil. The outcome is well-known. Christ himself illustrated the destiny of his message with the parable of the seed. The devil will steal it; it will be choked; it will wither (Mt. 13:1-23); but it will also occasionally be fruitful.

In this world there is a continuing struggle between good and evil; this also obtains within the people of God. For although Christ conquered the sovereign of this world, his influence was not completely destroyed. In the time between ascension and parousia we might say that God left him some power, but it is hobbled. The kingdom has a twofold phase — an earthly and a heavenly one and only in the latter will evil be completely voided. Christ illustrated this in the parable of the weeds and the wheat (Mt. 13:24-30). The farmer allows the weeds to grow. This irritated the servants, "No, do not pull them out! I am afraid that when you gather the weeds, you will root up the wheat along with them. Let both grow together until the harvest; and at harvest time I will tell the reapers, gather the weeds first and bind them in bundles to be burned, but gather the wheat into my barn." This means that God tolerates evil — he has good reasons for this — but he will terminate its power in the end.

When God condemns the evil one on the last day, he will at the same time reward the good.

This is the theme of the covenant promises. In the Old Covenant they were proclaimed at the same time as the Law. Christ does this too, but his method is only casually related to that in which the Old Testament promises were worded. Christ does it in the form of "beautification." To those who suffer many wrongs here on earth — this is God's rule — the kingdom of heaven is promised; very probably Christ refers to the kingdom of God in its end-phase, which is sometimes compared to a banquet. In this connection Matthew recalls the Old Testament that the meek will possess the promised land (cf. Ps. 37:11); in the light of the New Testament this is the heavenly homeland. For all who are

prepared for the kingdom of God, there will be no
more sadness, nor famine nor thirst. They will experience mercy at the judgment and will manifest
the sonship of God (Mt. 6:1-12).

Paul speaks of the redemption of the body (Rom.
8:23). To him this is the content of salvation expectations. "In this hope we are saved," he says.

And what comes after this earthly end-phase? The
visionary John tells us. "Then I saw a new heaven
and a new earth; for the first heaven and the first
earth had passed away, and the sea was no more.
And I saw the holy city, new Jerusalem, coming
down out of heaven from God, prepared as a bride
adorned for her husband; and I heard a great voice
from the throne saying, Behold, the dwelling of God
is with man. He will dwell with them, and they shall
be his people, and God himself will be with them;
he will wipe away every tear from their eyes, and
death shall be no more, neither shall there be
mourning nor crying nor pain anymore, for the
former things have passed away" (Rev. 21:1-4).
God's covenant salvation will be completely realized.

## 6.  God's love

Every covenant presupposes some degree of love.
When one partner brings great offerings to the other,
love is proportionately shown.

It sounds strange, but God brings such an offering
through the sacrifice of Jesus Christ. Christian literature sees the crucifixion as the tremendous sign of

love from Christ and from God. Paul has this concept. He asks the Romans not to insult their weak brothers, and gives as his motive the fact that Christ died for them (Rom. 14:15; cf. 1 Cor. 8:11). He says of himself that Christ loved him and gave himself for him (cf. Gal. 2:20). He presents Christ as an example for married men: "Husbands, love your wives, as Christ loved the Church and gave himself up for her . . ." (Eph. 5:25).

Christ's love is the revelation of God's love; he is the incarnated love of the invisible God. "But God shows his love for us in that, while we were yet sinners, Christ died for us" (Rom. 5:8; cf. Rom. 8:32; Jn. 3:16 etc.).

Paul sees another proof of God's love in the possession of the Spirit. In Rom. 5:5 he says, "And hopes do not disappoint us, because God's love has been poured into our hearts through the Holy Spirit which has been given to us." Is this a love directed to God or love coming from God, originating with him? Naturally, here the love which comes from God is emphasized. The Spirit which is given us and is the guarantee of glory, is the greatest proof of this.

## 7. The celebration of the covenant

On the eve of his passion, Christ pointed to the covenant renewing power of his crucifixion and invited his people to commemorate this offering. He established a sacramental and sacrificial celebration so that man would not forget the offering that re-

conciled him with God. He gave this remembrance
celebration the likeness of a meal.

As baptism was a symbolic representation of the
death and the resurrection of Christ, so is this
Eucharistic meal. The bread indicates his Body,
which is to be given up; the wine is the Blood which
is shed. In its whole manner of representation this
attitude of Christ reminds us of the sacrificial death
of Calvary. Conversely, bread and wine are life-
giving elements and point to the Risen Lord, the
life-giving Spirit. However, there is this difference
between baptism and the Eucharistic meal: Christ
is personally represented in the meal.

The people of Israel knew similar religious meals.
They had long celebrated a remembrance meal, the
pasch, which was a vivid reminder of their delivery
from the bondage of Egypt.

In Israel they were aware of the fact that this was
not only a past historical incident; it is still operative. The deliverance of the fathers was the source
of their present freedom. The Talmud reflects this
exactly: "Every generation has the duty to consider
itself as if it personally had gone out of Egypt."[16]
Christian antiquity saw the Eucharistic meal as
a fulfillment of the Jewish passover. This follows
the intention of Christ very well, for he established
this meal to take the place of the Jewish pasch. This
Easter-meal of Christ is a remembrance of our deliverance from the slavery of sin and death. His
own death accomplished this. "For as often as you

eat this bread and drink the cup, you proclaim the
Lord's death until he comes" (1 Cor. 11:26).

Israel knew a sacrificial meal. In Ex. 24:9-11 we
hear how the leaders of the people ate in the
presence of the Lord. They considered that God
himself was represented and imparted his favors
to them. He gave them his peace. The Eucharist
is also a fulfillment of this peace-meal. Christ is
really represented here. When we eat the bread
and drink from the cup, we enter into personal
contact with the Lord, we participate more and more
in the Spirit of the heavenly Christ. We grow close
to him, and are more and more influenced by his
life. John relates the words of Christ: "He who eats
my flesh and drinks my blood abides in me, and I in
him" (Jn. 6:56).

The New Covenant is a partnership in the life
of God, on the strength of our alliance with Jesus
Christ; on this we base our hope of glory with him.
The Eucharistic food lets us grow into a close
alliance with him. We say to him, "We belong to
you!" and he answers, "You are mine!"

# REFERENCES

1. P. Karge, "Geschichte des Bundesgedankes im Alten Testament" (*Alttestamentliche Abhandlungen* II, 1-4). Munster 1910, p. 239 ff.

2. W. F. Albright in *Bulletin of the American Schools of Oriental Research* 141 (1951) p. 21 ff. Th. C. Vriezen, *Theologie des Alten Testaments*, Neukirchen 1956, p. 116. E. Vogt, "Vox *berit* concrete adhibita," in *Biblica* 36 (1955) p. 566.

3. J. Pedersen, *Der Eid bei den Semiten*, Leipzig 1914, p. 31.

4. De Bazuin, 25 juni 1960, p. 6.

5. W. Eichrodt, *Theologie des Alten Testaments*, Gottingen 1959, p. 6.

6. G. von Rad, *Theologie des Alten Testaments* I, München 1958, p. 136.

7. W. Eichrodt, l.c. p. 14.

8. *De Bijbel over Heilsgeschiedenis*, by Fr. Stier, Roermond 1960, p. 40.

9. G. Ernest Wright, *Biblical Archaeology*, Philadelphia, Westminster Press, 1957, p. 112 ff.

10. Thus R. Kraetzschmar, R. Smend and B. Stade.

11. P. van Imschoot, *Theologie de l'Ancien Testament* I, Paris 1954, p. 244 V. Hamp, "Bund" in *Lexikon fur Theologie und Kirche*.

12. W. Grossouw, *Bijbelse vroomheid*, Utrecht 1954, p. 167.

13. W. Grossouw, l.c. p. 168.

14. R. Guardini, *Gebed en waarheid*, Hilversum 1961, p. 38.

15. R. Guardini l.c. p. 39.

16. Strack-Billerbeck, *Kommentar zum Neuen Testament aus Midrasch und Talmud*, München 1928, IV, I, p. 68.